An Investigation of Training Certified Substitute Teachers and What They Say Is Needed
to Be Effective in the Classroom

A Dissertation

Submitted to the
Faculty of Argosy University/Chicago
in partial fulfillment of
the requirements for the degree of
Doctor of Education
By

Yvonne Henderson

Argosy University/Chicago

July 2011

Dissertation Committee Approval:

_____

Dissertation Chair: Dr. Deborah Hammond-Watts   Date

_____

Committee Member: Dr. Florine Robinson

_____

Committee Member: Dr. Cheryl J. Richardson

_____

Program Chair: Dr. Tim Brown

Dedication

This dissertation is dedicated to my parents the late Rev. Wayde, Sr. & Ruth Ann Henderson, who always taught me to never give up. May they rest in peace. To my loving and supportive son, Laronne Latrell Walters, who always understood when I needed to study.

Acknowledgements

First, I would like to thank my Heavenly Father, God Almighty, who is the Source of my life, for always having my back, my front and everything in between and around. If it had not been for the Lord, I would not have made it this far. I have accomplished something that some said was impossible, but on the prayers of my family and friends, I have made it. With God all things are possible, I honestly believe "I can do all things through Christ who strengthens me" Philippians 4:13 (King James Version).

This has been a long journey not only for me, but for my son as well. He has sacrificed a lot of time with mommy to allow me to be able to reach this level of education. My hope and prayer are that he will understand the importance of education and follow in mommy's footsteps one day. Laronne I love you more than you will ever know, but I want to say thank you for being patient with me while I traveled down this long road. It is over and now we can enjoy the fruits of our labor.

To my family, thank you for your support and prayers, for the long conversations to help me stay focused, for the assistance with understanding that which I already knew and did not realize. To my haters, to God be the glory for the things He has done.

I would like to sincerely thank my committee, Dr. Deborah Hammond-Watts for being a wonderful Chair, Dr. Cheryl Richardson and Dr. Florine Robinson for being on my committee and providing your support and honesty when I needed it. To the Harvey

School District 152 without your support and help this study would not have been

possible.

Last, but not least my church family Union Evangelistic Baptist Church for always

praying for me when I felt like I could not go on. May God continue to bless and keep

you all. In the words of Jesus, "It is finished" John 30a. (KJV)

Abstract

     The educational system has gone through several changes over the years. In recent years, the Bush Administration developed The No Child Left Behind Act (NCLB), a mandate that required all educators to be highly qualified in the area being taught. This mandate was for teachers, administrators, and paraprofessionals. However, substitute teachers were not included. Teachers complained that no work was accomplished when a substitute teacher was in the room. Teachers felt substitute teachers were lacking in classroom management, (i.e. keeping order, discipline, handling emergencies, and delivering a lesson). This study investigated a certified substitute teacher training program of a school district in the south suburbs of a large metropolitan area. A self-administered questionnaire survey was administered and completed by district substitute teachers who had attended the districts training program. After compiling the data from the questionnaire survey's, using tables and charts the data showed substitute teachers had a lot to say about what they felt was needed in training to be effective in the classroom. The recommendations for substitute teacher training programs and further studies were made based on the data gathered from the questionnaire surveys.

List of Tables

Table

1   Demographic Characteristics of Respondents in the Study 47

2   Building Procedures/Gender Importance...51

2.1   Building Procedures/Race Importance...54

2.2   Building Procedures/Grades Taught – Importance 57

2.3   Building Procedures/ Years of Substituting – Importance...........................60

2.4   Building Procedures/Types of Substituting – Importance...........................65

2.5   Building Procedures/Trained Substitutes – Importance...............................68

3   Training/Gender Importance 71

3.1   Training/Race Importance 74

3.2   Training/Grades Taught – Importance...77

3.3   Training/Years of Substituting – Importance 81

3.4   Training/Type of Substituting – Importance...85

3.5   Training/Trained Substitutes – Importance 87

4   Classroom Management/Gender Importance 89

4.1   Classroom Management/Race Importance 91

4.2   Classroom Management/Grades Taught – Importance 93

4.3   Classroom Management/Years of Substituting – Importance 95

4.4   Classroom Management/Types of Substituting – Importance........................97

4.5   Classroom Management/Trained Substitutes – Importance............................99

5   Classroom Procedures/Gender Importance..101

5.1 Classroom Procedures/Race Importance 102

v

5.2   Classroom Procedures/Grades Taught – Importance 104

5.3   Classroom Procedures/Years of Substituting...106

5.4   Classroom Procedures/Type of Substituting – Importance 109

5.5   Classroom Procedures/Trained Substitutes – Importance......................................111

List of Charts

Chart 1 Building Procedures/ Top questions of Importance ……………..…………….…….114

Chart 2 Training/ Top questions of Importance ……………………………………………115

Chart 3 Classroom Management/ Top questions of Importance ...………………………..116

Chart 4 Classroom Procedures/ Top questions of Importance ………………………….. 116

Table of Contents

Dedication ………………………………………………………………i

Acknowledgements ……………………………………………………..ii

Abstract …………………………………….....................................iv

List of Tables …………………………………………………… v

List of Charts …………………………………………………….vi

Chapter

   I.   THE PROBLEM …………………………………………......1

       Introduction ……………………………………………… 1

           Purpose ………………………………………………….5

           Conceptual Framework ……………………………………...6

           Definitions ……………………………………………….7

           Preview of Literature …………………………………….8

           Preview of Methodology …………………………………11

           Significance of the Study ……………………………...…12

           Assumptions ……………………………………………12

           Limitations …………………………………………….13

           Delimitations …………………………………………...13

           Summary of Chapter One ………………………………13

   II. LITERATURE REVIEW …………………………………15

           Introduction...…………………………………………15

           Increased Use of Substitutes…………………………….16

Management of Substitute Teachers ……………………………………21

Effectiveness …………………………………………………………..24

Hiring ……………………………………………………………………26

Retaining ……………………………………………………………27

Training ………………………………………………………………28

Summary of Chapter Two ………………………………………31

III. METHODOLOGY ……………………………………………34

Introduction ……………………………………………………34

Design ……………………………………………………………35

Population and Sample ……………………………………35

Setting ……………………………………………………………36

Instrumentation ……………………………………………..36

Questioning ……………………………………………………36

Procedures ………………………………………………………...39

Questionnaire Survey Data Collection ……………………………41

Summary of Chapter Three …………………………………………42

IV. FINDINGS AND ANALYSIS OVERVIEW …………………………43

Data Collection Procedures …………………………………………43

Population ……………………………………………………44

The Instrument ………………………………………………45

Results of the Analysis …………………………………………46

Demographic Respondents ……………………………………..47

Categories of Importance ……………………………………48

Building Procedures ……………………………………48

Gender ………………………………………………………49

Race …………………………………………………………52

Grades Taught ………………………………………………55

Years Substituting …………………………………………58

Type of Substituting ………………………………………...62

Trained Substitutes …………………………………………67

Training …………………………………………………69

Gender ………………………………………………………71

Race …………………………………………………………72

Grades Taught ………………………………………………75

Years Substituting …………………………………………78

Type of Substituting ………………………………………..82

Trained Substitutes …………………………………………86

Classroom Management ………………………………88

Gender ……………………………………………………...89

Race ………………………………………………………...90

Grades Taught ………………………………………………92

Years Substituting …………………………………………94

Type of Substituting ………………………………………96

Trained Substitutes …………………………………………98

Classroom Procedures 99

Gender 100

Race...102

Grades Taught 103

Years Substituting 104

Type of Substituting 107

Trained Substitutes 110

Open-ended Question Responses 111

Summary of Chapter Four...112

V. INTRODUCTION, DISCUSSION, RECOMMENDATIONS, AND SUMMARY 117

Introduction 117

Summary of the Study 117

Discussion 123

Recommendations for Training Programs 128

Recommendations for further research 129

Summary of Chapter Five...130

Appendix

A. Self-Administered Questionnaire Survey Cover 132

Self-Administered Questionnaire Survey ....

B. Recruitment Script Cover 137

xi

Recruitment Script ....

C. Informed Consent to Participate in Research Cover 138

Informed Consent to Participate in Research ....

D. Permission Letter from Harvey School District 152 Cover 143

Permission Letter from Harvey School District 152 ....

E. CITI Collaborative Institutional Completion Report Cover 145

CITI Collaborative Institutional Completion Report ....

F. Institutional Review Board Approval Cover 147

Institutional Review Board Approval ....

REFERENCES...145

CHAPTER ONE: THE PROBLEM

Introduction

Being an educator is one of the most fulfilling things one could ever do. Being able to impart knowledge, inspire, and enlighten students daily has proven to be an extra ordinary task to say the least. Before reaching this thrilling conclusion, the researcher had to reach a level of appreciation for the art of teaching. Being a certified substitute teacher for two years, in three different school districts, while working on teacher certification the researcher was exposed to several issues that lead to conducting this study. Upon entering a regular teachers' classroom as a substitute teacher the researcher found this was not as easy as it seemed to appear; trying to accomplish what the regular classroom teacher provided proved to be a little more difficult than expected, without the proper training to be in a classroom. Ezarik (2004) says, "Many well-educated people "who are competent and would do well on a temporary basis [in schools] know better than to put themselves in harm's way by walking into a classroom" (p. 32). Noticing some things as a substitute teacher and a regular classroom teacher led to this investigation of a substitute training program.

First, teachers would not leave adequate lesson plans. For example: On several occasions regular classroom teachers would leave instructions for students to read a passage and answer the questions that follow. This seems to be an easy lesson to follow, but what ensued next was far from easy. Student's would say they finished that assignment the day before, which, would leave a substitute teacher feeling less than prepared for the day, Javernick (2005) states, substitutes lose credibility when students are able to triumphantly, say "We did that yesterday!" (p.47). Or fifteen minutes into a one-hour class period student's claim to have completed the assignment, leaving forty-five minutes of uninstructed time, without other materials left by the regular classroom teacher.

Second were the complaints of students. After becoming a regular classroom teacher trying to create lessons that were different from the previous days' work, whenever possible, to keep students from saying it had been completed the day before was something this researcher strived to do. Then another problem surfaced that really made the researcher to embark on this topic; the student complaints were overwhelming about substitutes not doing anything. The students would say that the substitute did nothing but hand out the assignment, surf the web or read the newspaper, and drink coffee. Certified substitute teachers should be highly qualified and held to the same standards as the regular classroom teacher to continue the educational process of the students. Ballard (2005) says, districts need to aggressively address training substitute teachers to develop highly qualified substitute teachers.

Third substitute teachers should follow the lesson plans provided. After returning to work from a district caused leave, or a teacher caused leave it was difficult to know

2

what was accomplished by the substitute teacher and what was not. Student work was not graded, even though answer keys were prepared in advance. Student work was lost or misplaced. On average it took the researcher approximately two or three days to get assignments back on track after having a substitute teacher for just one day. Haas states (as cited by Ezarik, 2004) teaching is the only profession that allows substitutes without training to stand in for a professional. Without proper training these types of situations will continue to occur.

Lastly, how little substitute teachers were appreciated was a concern. Upon entering one school the question was asked "Who are you today?" as if a substitute teacher did not have an identity. Ezarik (2004) points out some suggestions for making a substitute teacher feel welcomed in your district: 1) Good first impressions, do not be a nightmare administrator. 2) Be affectionate, show the substitute teacher you care by celebrating them during National Substitute Teacher Recognition Week. 3) Show up and help the substitute teacher get acclimated to the classroom. 4) Be encouraging of personal and professional growth by giving incentives for continued education courses. 5) Be personable, know the substitute teachers name and address them by their name.

These are just a few of the reasons why the investigation of training substitute teachers and what they say is needed to be effective in the classroom was so important. Due to a lack of understanding the ins and outs of the educational system certified substitute teachers are not viewed as educators and are not treated with the same respect

3

as regular classroom teachers from administrators, other teachers, and students.

Certification is a way to show teachers are qualified to teach in a area, and on-going training is required for all certified teachers to remain effective in their perspective field. In recent years teachers have been mandated because of A Nation at Risk, and the No Child Left Behind Act (NCLB) to acquire continuing education credits by attending professional development seminars, conferences, workshops, and other training (Wyld, 1995). Certified substitute teachers should be held to the same standards. With teachers out of the classroom more the need to secure certified substitute teachers increased. If through this reform teaching and learning is to truly improve, substitute teachers need to be added to the professional learning perceived and executed by educators (Lamarque, 2005).

The qualifications for substitute teachers vary from state to state. In 2010 The National Education Association (NEA) reported, in Alabama, Alaska, Florida, Georgia, Idaho, Maine, South Dakota, Vermont, and Virginia substitute teachers only need a high school diploma to fill in for an absent certified teacher. In Indiana, Missouri, Nebraska, New Jersey, Nevada, and Wyoming, substitute teachers were required to have a minimum of 60-65 college credit hours to fill in for an absent certified teacher. States that required substitute teachers to have a bachelor's degree, or be certified were; California, Colorado, Connecticut, Illinois, Iowa, Kansas, Massachusetts, Minnesota, Mississippi, Nevada, North Dakota, Oregon, and West Virginia. Other states not mentioned did not have a minimum requirement for substitute teachers, but stated they followed state guidelines. Lamarque (2005) found that "the services of a dependable, well-prepared substitute are essential to providing continuity in student academic achievement" (p. 11).

In 1995 the Substitute Teaching Institute at Utah State University (STI/USU) came into existence; their focus was on substitute teachers and the skills needed to be effective in the classroom. STI/USU has set up and maintained a program geared solely to substitute teachers. STI/USU are on the cutting edge of this problem and are continually making changes to their program for the betterment of substitute teachers.

Research shows that over the course of a twelve-year school period students will be taught by a substitute teacher for the equivalent of one school year. Honawar (2007) found that on an average day 8-10 percent of classrooms are staffed with a substitute teacher, which equates to approximately 274,000 substitute teachers in our nation's classrooms in just one day. Lawmakers have come to realize that having trained substitute teachers are a problem as well. NCLB Act originally only addressed substitute teachers who held long-term positions the NCLB Act is being re-evaluated to incorporate specific requirements for all substitute teachers (Honawar, 2007).

Purpose

The purpose of this study was to investigate a substitute teacher training program to ascertain from the substitute teachers if the training received is helpful in them being effective in the classroom. Past research on this topic has been generated by individual school districts, government agencies, and education associations from the perspective of the school districts, administrators, and teacher's, however, extraordinarily little input is given from the perspective of the substitute teacher. This study focused on gaining the perspective of the substitute teacher as to what they say is needed in training to be effective in the classroom

In the 2010 report submitted by the National Education Association (NEA), over half of the states in the United States did not have a training program for substitute teachers. This report helps to solidify the purpose for this study. Investigating the effectiveness of a training program for certified substitute teachers from the certified substitute teachers' perspective was the catch to this study, from this direction there is a paucity in the literature. This study focused on the gap in the literature to answer the following question: What do substitute teachers say is needed from substitute teacher training to be effective in the classroom?

Conceptual Framework

For this study, a mixed method with the quantitative study focusing on a survey research design and an open-ended question to address the quantitative data was chosen. Leedy and Ormrod (2005) states, that survey research is used to obtain information from one or more groups of people, by asking questions and tabulating responses. To gain information about characteristics, opinions, attitudes, and or prior experiences of certified substitute teachers a survey was developed and used. A set of questions were generated to be answered by the participants; they were cross tabulated and summarized with percentages. This approach has been used in many areas of human activity. This was the same method used when obtaining information from individuals and political candidates with the Gallup Poll.

Definitions

Certified Substitute Teacher: Replacing a certified teacher with one of equal value (Purvis & Garvey, 1993).

Classroom Management: A strategic plan on how to deal with discipline, order in the classroom, school policy and procedures (Javernick, 2005).

District Caused Absence: Teacher leave for professional development, workshops, etc. (Koelling, 1983).

Effectiveness: Systematic construct for directing change in professional practice (Guskey & Sparks, 1991).

Floater: an employee who works at various times, locations, etc. as required by an employer

(Webster, 2010).

Highly Qualified Substitute: A person well versed in the techniques that produce an effective classroom in which the educational process continues during the regular teacher's absence (Ballard, 2005).

Interim Teacher: A person with approximately the same duties and responsibilities as a regular teacher (Lassmann, 2001).

Long Term Substitute: Being in a class for 21 consecutive days or longer at one time (Honawar, 2007).

Permanent: Not expected to change in status, condition, or place (Webster, 2010).

Program Evaluation: Collection of information about the activities, characteristics, and outcomes of a program (Patton, 2002).

Short Term Substitute: Replacing a teacher for 10-14 days (NEA, 2010).

SubManagers: Personnel that contacts substitute teachers (Haines, 2005).

Teacher Caused Absence: Teacher leave for illness, bereavement, personal leave, etc. (Koelling, 1983).

Preview of Literature

In searching the literature for the effectiveness of training programs from the certified substitute teacher's perspective there was truly little. What is a substitute teacher? Purvis & Garvey (1993) states a certified substitute teacher is a replacement for a certified teacher with equal values. But are they equal? When one thinks of a substitute something less than what one really wants comes to mind. A knock off, something not quite as good as the real thing, something you get at the last minute. Based on the literature substitute teachers feel like less of a person when substituting in some districts because substitute teachers were not treated in a respectful manner.

Shaw (1998) recalls being a substitute teacher and reflecting on why she was a substitute teacher, she felt her job was to fill in for the teacher who was absent; sometimes she was the answer to an emergency, left with incomplete, or no plans at all. Shaw began substitute teaching in hopes of one day having her own classroom. Shaw goes on to say, "…When I come into your classroom to teach your students in your absence, I expect not to baby-sit, but teach" (p.60).

Warner (2003) recalls accepting a long-term substitute teaching assignment for a 6th grade class. He was fingerprinted, had a background check done, and watched an instructional video on how to handle spilled bodily fluids and then shown to the classroom. This has been the extent of some of the training that has been given to substitute teachers across the country. In some cases, substitute teachers are given a two-hour course.

In a 1983 study Koelling found for many years the use of substitute teachers in schools received little attention. "Even though the subject has been addressed more in recent years there remains a paucity of attention in relation to the importance of the issues involved" (p. 155). The literature gives a few alternatives as to the instructional problems caused by a teacher's absence and use of substitute teachers. Koelling (1983) concluded

9

that any efforts taken should first clearly address the role and expectations of the substitute teacher, to recognize their importance in the instructional process, and to train them. More of Koelling's study will be discussed in Chapter Two.

Lassmann (2001) suggests, renaming substitute teachers and call them "interim" teachers. When replacing a principal, superintendent, or university president they are referred to as 'Interim' superintendent, or 'Interim' president. Giving substitute teachers a better way to view themselves will make it much easier for them to be accepted and taken seriously. It may even boost morale or allow substitute teachers to receive the level of respect of the certified teacher being replaced, (Lassmann, 2001).

In 2010 the Illinois State Board of Education (ISBE) website states the qualifications for being a substitute teacher are minimal. The federal government's only requirement for a substitute teacher in a Title 1 school is that the parents be notified if a certified substitute will be in the classroom long-term. Most districts see long-term as 21 consecutive school days or more. At this point there are 29 states that have a minimum requirement for substitute teachers that were listed earlier. Although 10 percent of substitute teachers have the minimum requirement, a third are certified substitute teachers, and another third have bachelor's degrees. However, still some 90 percent of substitute teachers do not receive formal training (Honawar, 2007). The bottom line is that in many districts 100 percent of substitute teachers are not qualified to be in our nation's classrooms. Some school boards do not want to provide training for substitute teachers, but districts spend 3.8 billion a year on substitute teachers (Dyri 2004).

Other studies conducted by Fielder (1991), and Haines (2005) will be discussed in depth by in Chapter Two. These studies provide information about substitute teacher programs and their effectiveness, however there was little feedback from substitute teachers, which is why this study was done.

Preview of Methodology

It is known that data collection is important to any research study. The way data is collected has a varied impact on the evaluation of any study. There are quantitative methods on one hand and qualitative methods on the other hand; most recently there has been the use of the mixed method. The selected design chosen for this study was a mixed method with a quantitative research study and an open-ended question for the qualitative portion. In conducting this study a self-administered questionnaire survey was used and administered to certified substitute teachers to obtain their perspective on the training received from their school district and what certified substitutes say is needed in the training to be effective in the classroom. Approximately 100 certified substitute teachers were to be surveyed. Upon approval for the study certified substitute teachers in a suburban of a large metropolitan area school district with a certified substitute teacher training program were invited to take part in the study. In using a quantitative method of data collection, a purposeful sample fit the experience. This allowed summarizing and comparisons to be easier (The University of Wisconsin EAU CLAIRE, 2009).

The survey utilized in this study was to get an idea of what the certified substitute teachers say is needed from the training to be effective in the classroom. Surveys are a good way to explore what people are thinking. Surveys can be used to obtain specific information gathered to confirm interpretations in other forms of data collection.

Significance of the study

This study is significant in professional development for certified substitute teachers and the educational system, and it contributes to the literature by giving the certified substitute teachers a voice. The study also addressed the gap in the literature about the substitute teacher's viewpoint of what is needed to be effective in the classroom. After conducting this research project, a better perspective on training for certified substitute teachers from their perspective on how to be more effective has been established.

Assumptions

Assumptions in this study were that certified substitute teachers have some knowledge of classroom expectations and should know what is expected for a successful day. It is also assumed that there is some training being given to certified substitute teachers. It is also assumed that the certified substitute teachers are getting something needed from the training programs in their school district.

Limitations/Delimitations

Survey Limitations

In conducting this study, the limitations or things that are not controlled by the researcher are as follows: The survey cannot be sent through the mail due to the privacy act for employees. Emails could not be used because emails are only used for district related information.

Delimitations

In conducting this study, the delimitations or things that can be controlled by the researcher are as follows: One school district in a large metropolitan urban area was chosen for the study. Another delimitation that was acknowledged is only using certified substitute teachers who had gone through the districts substitute teacher training program would be surveyed.

Summary

Chapter one was insightful, it explained the qualifications needed to become a substitute teacher in several states. Chapter one also explained the purpose of this study, which was to find out what certified substitute teachers say is needed in training to be effective in the classroom. The brief literature review showed the gap in the literature from the certified substitute teacher's perspective, the preview of the methodology

13

addressed what was used to collect the data needed for this study. The limitations of using a survey and delimitations of only selecting on cite for the study. Chapter one also addressed the significance of this study and how this study would contribute to the professional development of certified substitute teachers. Chapter two will provide an in-depth review of studies that point out the gap in the literature from the certified substitute teachers' perspectives on training programs.

CHAPTER TWO: REVIEW OF THE LITERATURE

Introduction

In researching the history of substitute teacher training the one thing that constantly came up was The Substitute Teaching Institution at Utah State University (STI/USU). Founded in 1995 they began supplying substitute teachers with educational materials on "how-tos" and fill-in activities. Since inception it has evolved into the leader of improving substitute teachers. In 1997 the U.S. Department of Education awarded the university federal funding for field-initiated research in the area of substitute teaching. STI/USU continues to design training materials and services to enhance the quality of substitute teachers.

Substitute teachers are needed for school districts around the globe. Honawar (2007) found a teacher shortage across the United States which is requiring more and more substitute teachers. Qualifications for hiring substitute teachers vary from state to state. Some states only require a high school diploma or GED, some require 60 credit hours, some require a four-year degree, and most do not even require training. In the following literature review studies will show other elements that are important as to why this study was done.

In investigating the effectiveness of certified substitute teachers training programs it was difficult due to the paucity in the literature. Very few current studies on training

15

programs for certified substitute teachers from the certified substitute teacher's perspective were found. Chapter twos literature review addressed the purpose of the study outlined in Chapter one. The review looked at training programs for substitute teachers. Other areas focused on were: Increased use of substitute teachers, management of substitute teachers, and the effectiveness of substitute teachers. Subareas discussed are hiring, retaining, and training of certified substitute teachers.

The Increased Use of Substitutes

For many years little attention was paid to the growing concerns of substitute teacher use in schools. In recent years more has been done, however, there is still a gap in the literature Koelling (1983). Koelling, 1983 conducted a qualitative study using the questionnaire patterned after The Educational Research Service study conducted in 1977 which investigated the policies and practices that would determine the direction and effectiveness of substitute teacher programs with 1,158 schools across the United States that had a pupil enrollment of 300 or more.

Koelling (1983) developed a questionnaire based on a lack of information in the literature. Formed questions were submitted to four professors of Educational Administration and piloted with six central office school administrators. Upon completion of these two stages he felt the response were good enough to continue with the questionnaire. The final questionnaire consisted of twenty-three questions and sub-areas dealing with "Administrative Arrangements, Qualifications, and Operation"

16

(p.156). The questionnaire was distributed to a few schools in the nineteenth state region governed by the North Central Association of Colleges and Schools.

The sample size was 5,867 Kindergarten or one to twelfth grade districts. They were then put into categories by enrollment. The goal was to obtain a minimum of twenty percent from large districts and 100% in low population schools. A large school district would consist of a population of 100 or more students enrolled, five schools were chosen. Smaller districts had a student population of 100 or less. The categories were divided as follows: 1-999; 1,000-4,999; 5,000-9,999; 10,000 and more. All the schools in the highest categories were sent questionnaires, 37.6 percent were sent to the schools in the 1,000-4,999 category, 25.4 percent to schools in the 1-999 category. In all 2,123 districts were mailed questionnaires, 1,728 or 81.39 percent of questionnaires returned were useable. Participants were instructed to answer all questions they could but omit any questions that could not be answered adequately. Answers for each question varied and, in each instance, answers were slightly or very much less than the total numbers of questionnaires returned (Koelling, 1983).

It was quite compelling that the data showed only 10.8 percent of the districts had written contracts for substitute teachers while 89.2 percent of districts did not have written contracts for substitute teachers. It was more likely for larger districts to have written contracts compared to smaller districts. Interesting enough many districts required regular teachers to have health certificates due to close contact with students. Koelling,

1983 was extremely interested in knowing if the same held true for substitute teachers. Based on the data only 32.7 percent of all districts required substitutes to have a health certificate; twice as likely in districts with 5,000 or more enrolled than those districts with less than 5,000.

With substitute teachers being utilized so often Koelling, 1993 wanted to know how substitutes were being paid day by day or by the hour. Almost universally the data paid substitute teachers by the day; 99.8 percent. Koelling, 1983 revealed that some districts felt substitute teachers should be considered "full time" teachers after working a certain amount of time for salary purposes. Only two-thirds of all districts followed the practice and only in districts with enrollment of 1,000 or more students. Within those districts the range of days worked was very widespread. It ranged from three to ninety-nine, 65.8% required ten and thirty days before a substitute teacher would be considered to receive regular teacher pay. The data showed that 6.7% said substitute teacher receive fringe benefits, and in large districts 16.7% paid fringe benefits. The Educational Research Study (as cited in Koelling, 1983) reported approximately 25% paid fringe benefits in 1977. With the way the economy is today one would find it more likely to provide fringe benefits now as oppose to back in 1977.

To obtain the best replacement for regular teachers Koelling, 1983 wanted to know the selection process of obtaining substitute teachers. Four out of five districts said they had a substitute teacher "pool". The range was "three in four for smaller districts to about nine in ten for larger districts" (p. 158). Koelling (1983) says, "Screening and approval of people to be in the substitute teacher pool will probably have some impact upon quality and output" (p. 159).

With the increase of regular teachers taking off it is only fitting to know how often substitute teachers are used in a year. Only 1,136 districts answered this question providing a fair basis for analysis. To give useful meaning to the data a ratio of substitute teacher days used with the number of teachers was constructed. The ranges were calculated as follows: "one day per year per teacher to twenty-nine days per year per teacher, 94.7% reported substitute teacher days per teacher from one to ten with this the data was only used to reflect that limit. 62.2% of smaller districts used five or less substitute teacher days per regular teacher and 60.5 % of the largest districts used five or more. With this information Koelling, 1983 sought to find out how often substitute teachers were used. Were they used for teacher caused (illness, personal leave, etc.) or district caused (professional development, workshops, etc.)? One thousand forty-one districts answered the question about teacher caused absence and 833 about district caused absences. To get an accurate analysis raw data was complied to create a comparison based on substitute teacher days per regular teacher employed.

Koelling (1993), states in recent years districts have tried to change the way in-services are attended by not having all personnel attend at one time, thus not needing to use as many substitute teachers per day. The data concluded the greatest number of

19

districts that used one substitute teacher day per regular teacher for district caused absences. On the other hand, one in four used two or more days per regular teacher. Larger districts used two or more days than smaller districts.

With more and more substitute teachers being used qualifications of substitute teachers was another concern of Koelling, 1993. While qualifications vary for substitute teachers, qualifications would have some effect on the quality of service rendered from the substitute teacher (Koelling, 1983). Koelling, 1983 found three out of four districts required substitute teachers to have a substitute teacher certificate or a regular teacher certificate. Amazingly enough 25% of the two smaller enrollment categories did not have this requirement. When asked about college hours most said yes in three out of four of the largest enrollment groups. There was a wide range of requirements from thirty, sixty, or on hundred twenty hours were required. Having previous teaching experience was not a requirement for any of the districts.

Koelling (1983) looked at how districts secured, assigned, oriented, and evaluated substitute teachers', he explored the role played by teachers, building principals and central office personnel in this process. In selecting substitute teachers 80% of districts said teachers had no say, while 20% of districts say teachers do. Nine out of ten districts reported, regular teachers request for a substitute teacher is honored as much as possible. The process for contacting substitute teachers were secured by building principals in two out of three cases, but it was one of eight in the largest districts. Most districts tried to place substitute teachers by training, experience, and grade level whenever possible, success was made in one half of the cases.

As far as formal orientation programs one in ten are used in small districts and six in ten in the largest districts. Out of the 1,566 districts 421 had formal orientation programs, 331 were conducted by the central office, 208 were conducted at the building level, and 98 were conducted by both. One in four districts had formal evaluation plans, but at the larger districts it was more of a 50-50 chance that a formal evaluation was in place for substitute teachers. In evaluating the substitute teachers there were 831 responses of that 13 said students, 86 said central office 287 said teachers, 421 said building principals, and 14 were other. When asked how often the response was not good, 114 districts, 26.4% said once a year, 50 or 11.6% said twice a year, and 268 or 62% were other. Koelling, 1983 found these relationships to be statistically significant ($p => .01$) "The most compelling summary which can be made about the foregoing data is that most school districts do not have, in place, a comprehensive systematic and effective substitute teacher program" (p.171).

Management of Substitute Teachers

There are thousands of substitute teachers being used daily throughout the country, and management of substitute teachers are a growing concern. To gain a better understanding of the growing phenomena Haines conducted a qualitative study, in 2005

21

using a five-question telephone survey with administrators. The purpose of the study was to see how their substitute teacher program was going. The areas covered in the telephone survey were: Important topics that should be covered verbally with substitute teachers before employment. What are some improvement areas for substitute teachers to be more proficient? What type of screening procedures is in place for substitute teachers? What practices are used to manage substitute teachers, and what changes need to be made to the current districts substitute teacher programs?

Targeted administrators for the study were: Substitute Coordinators, Directors of Human Resources, Staff Development Directors, or Personnel Directors. Selection of participants was in a voluntary basis. Out of the 50 states contacted 33 states responded and there was a total of 126 participants in the study. Student enrollment for the districts represented ranged from 173 students in three schools to 209,700 students in 293 schools.

The results to the question on topics discussed with substitute teachers before entering the classroom were somewhat biased based on the position of the administrator answering. A general orientation to help substitute teachers survive in the classroom and meet minimum district expectations was stated by 36.4% of the administrators. 27.3% of the districts had a seven-hour minimum training program. 18.2% said classroom management was the most important topic once all the paperwork was completed, and 11.6% stated sometimes they only cover state and district mandates (i.e. blood-borne pathogens and sexual harassment). Reasons were not given by districts why the topics covered were chosen or if feedback was supplied by substitute teachers as to how the topics covered helped in the classroom. Smith's study (As cited by Haines, 2005) states that, in 2000 90% of school districts nationwide training programs were two hours or less and 53% did not have training programs at all.

The study showed when administrators were asked about areas substitute teachers were least proficient, 67% said classroom management, 19% said teaching strategies and skills, and 13% said legal issues. This was the case regardless of educational background even in those districts that required substitute teachers to have teacher certificates, classroom management ranked high, but a percentage was not given. "Evidently certification is not a guarantee of teaching competency" (Haines, 2005, p. 36).

With the screening process of substitute teachers Haines, 2005 revealed that 22.6% of the districts said they used mandates by the state, "e.g., criminal background, fingerprints, etc." (p. 36). Some said, personal references, past employment, and/or educational verification. 30% of the participants conducted personal interviews. District and state-mandated training was another tool, however, only 5.6% of the districts surveyed had training prior to employment. Those using staffing agencies depended on the screening method uses by the agency.

Haines, 2005 reported over 75% of districts did not feel what they were doing in their substitute teacher program was innovative. Unfortunately, those who did feel they were using innovative techniques really did not know where the practices originated.

40% declared they came from the district, while 14% credited STI/USU.

The final question about changes to the substitute teacher program is truly relevant, it shows the paucity in the literature where the substitute teachers voice is not represented. Only one respondent said pay, for those substitute teachers doing an effective job in the classroom. 62% which was a majority said more training. With teachers out of the classroom Haines, 2005 validated the need of training substitute teachers to be more effective educators.

Effectiveness

"Everyone educated in this country has encountered substitute teachers during his or her years in school" (Fielder, 1991, p.1). In every field being effective is a key component to success. Teachers are held to a high standard of effectiveness to instruct students in the classroom and substitute teachers should be held to the same standard. In years past substitute teachers have rarely been objectively studied. When looking through the literature extraordinarily little on is available and that which is out there is based on opinion with no empirical basis. In the 1991 study Fielder conducted an objective exploratory study of substitute teachers to determine effectiveness. The purpose of the study was to explore the characteristics of effectiveness in substitute teachers. Participants were selected from a suburban/inner city southeastern school district with a student population of 5,000, approximately 65% of the students were white, 33% were black, and 2% other. The remainder was a low-income district with 38% of the students' population was eligible for free or reduced-price lunch; the rest of the student population was evenly split between middle and upper economic levels. There was one high school, one middle school, and two elementary schools involved in the study. A qualitative research method was used through a questionnaire, direct observation, open-ended interviews, and behavior-event interviews (BEI).

From the four schools selected six effective and six ineffective substitute teachers to participated in the study along with twelve regular classroom teachers; among the twelve were four regular teachers from the high school, four regular teachers from the middle school, and one principal at each level; elementary, middle school, and high school. Four substitute teachers from each school level were observed in the classroom. All the substitute teachers completed a questionnaire and participated in an open-ended interview session, and in a behavior-even interview, a technique developed by Castle. Substitute teachers were asked to describe instances where they believed they were most and least effective in the classroom. Using the BEI allows one to identify superior performance in their situations which would illustrate effective performance and critical behaviors to their job. The opposite of that would also be true.

To determine the effectiveness of the substitute teachers' evaluations of previous performance were utilized. Regular classroom teachers and principals who had used the substitute teachers' services completed a five-point Likert scale evaluation to rate the substitute teacher performance. To be considered effective a substitute teacher received a five in all categories on two or more evaluations. To be considered ineffective a substitute teacher received a rating of two on most of the categories on two or more evaluations, and the teachers and principals said they did not want this substitute teacher in their classroom or school again. The categories were not shared in the study, which created an even larger gap in what is expected of certified substitute teachers.

Fielder, 1991 yielded several characteristics of an effective and ineffective substitute teacher based on behavior and observation. Behavior characteristics were considered something that is directly observed. They are as follows: movement/monitoring, on-task concerns, physical touch, behavior expectation statement, personalizing, discipline-behaviors, and positive reinforcement. Some negative traits were sarcasm, and negativism (Fielder, 1991).

Observational characteristics that Fielder, 1991 found to determine a substitute teachers effectiveness or ineffectiveness in the classroom was: Dramaturgy, keeping students involved without embarrassing them, organization, adaptability, quick impression management, businesslike general demeanor, adult interpersonal skills, love, understanding, caring of children, humor, and internal motivation (Fielder, 1991). These characteristics were not placed in any sort of order but could be applied to the effectiveness or ineffectiveness of a substitute teacher.

Hiring

Dyrli (2004) found administrators are having a difficult time hiring substitute

26

teachers when teachers call off work. After taking on the task of calling substitute teachers for absent teacher's administrators felt there had to be a better way. After receiving several responses to an on-line inquiry, Dyrli, 2004 states, administrators found that getting substitute teachers were a difficult task and a continuing challenge around the country. Dyrli, 2004 found that Administrators spend $3.8 billion annually in the United States of America for substitute teachers, and that teachers were absent on average of 14-16 days a year. With high numbers of days missed by regular classroom teachers' students grades K-12 would have a substitute teacher for the equivalence of more than an academic year. With findings like this it is especially important to make sure our nations students are being taught by qualified substitute teachers.

In an effort to see what substitute teachers needed Smith reports (as cited in Ezarik, 2004) a survey was done in 1999 and asked questions like "Do you think you could effectively manage a classroom?", "Do you have concerns about being assigned to a special education class" (p.34)?

Retaining

Retaining substitute teachers in many districts is a large problem. For some districts, the main factor of the problem is the lack of pay and benefits. In a Denver school district, the substitute teacher pay was cut 67%. Substitute teacher pay would go from $121.45 per day to $81.54 (Keller, 2004). Smith (as cited in Lamarque, 2005) says to gain qualified substitute teachers' lower qualifications and more pay is not the answer.

Training is the key.

Training

Tannebaum (2000) looked at seven counties in New Jersey. Administrators, regular teachers, substitute teachers, and students were interviewed. The purpose of the study was to get a better understanding of what needed to be done to have qualified substitute teachers in the classroom. To acquire highly qualified substitute teachers the administrators felt substitute teachers who went through training should be paid more than those who did not go through training. The administrators also had concerns about classroom management and discipline when substitute teachers are in the classrooms. Both administrators and teachers felt that substitute teachers needed orientation. Teachers went on to say that substitute teachers do not follow the lesson plans left, and students did not get anything accomplished when a substitute teacher was in the classroom. Substitute teachers complained that not enough work was left to keep students occupied for the class period, and students were unruly. Students complained about substitute teachers who come in and just sit behind the desk and read the newspaper. There is a problem with the lack of training for substitute teachers. Another problem that surfaced from the literature was the reluctance of school boards to fund training for substitute teachers.

Honawar (2007) dealt with substitute teachers being highly qualified. He discusses how the government is trying to deal with the overwhelming need for qualified substitutes. Until recently federal lawmakers had not addressed substitute teachers in the

No Child Left Behind Act, "Only to "strongly" recommend that long term substitute teachers meet requirements for being "highly qualified" (p. 2), and the rights of the parents being informed when a substitute teacher was in the classroom of children in Title 1 schools. Another problem brought out in the literature was that the less qualified substitute teachers were found in high-poverty schools.

Jones (1999) described a meeting of 22 public school administrators and personnel directors who gathered to discuss the problems with substitute teachers and how to help. The meeting addressed four key topics as it related to what would make a qualified substitute teacher. Topics with the most concern were recruiting, and retaining, training, screening, and evaluating substitute teachers. Jones (1999) found school districts that had implemented training programs for substitute teachers increased the substitute teacher pool, decreased the number of complaints, and improved the quality of classroom instruction.

Lamarque (2005) states a positive and significant impact was made on the quality of education for students when the regular teacher was absent and substitute teachers were skilled; the substitute teacher acts more like a partner in the learning process, and it gives substitute teachers value and professional worth.

Lamarque, 2005 found that training substitute teachers "make them feel important, professional, confident, and valued" (p. 11), it has also given them more "respect from administrators, faculty, students, and parents" (p. 11).

In the 2005 study Gentry discussed training substitute teachers in Waco, Texas by the Education Service Center (ESC). With the new program training was given semiannually before the fall and spring semesters. Since 2003 over 700 substitute teachers have been trained. This came about after an investigation of the 12th Region. Abdal-Haqq, reports (as cited in Gentry, 2005) ESC found daily there were up to 10% of the nation's classrooms occupied with a substitute teacher. Longhurst study (as cited by Gentry, 2005) found 53% of districts did not have training for substitute teachers, and the 10% of districts that had training it was for 2 hours.

Other issues found by ESC (as cited by Gentry, 2005) substitute teachers were not treated like regular educators, substitute teachers did not feel like professionals based on the treatment received from teachers, students, and administrators. Jabbia says (as cited in Lamarque, 2005) the importance of substitute teachers needs to be reevaluated as to how they relate to students learning progress. Substitute teachers should be valued as a partnership and treated like professionals and allies with the school.

Abdal-Haqq, (as cited by Gentry, 2005) claimed that classroom management was the greatest challenge faced by substitute teachers. For some reason when a substitute teacher was in the room students felt this was a time to misbehave. Substitute teachers complained about lesson plans not being complete or missing all together. The literature also states that the low priority of training substitute teachers reflected the responses from teachers and students, which were also documented to be a problem some 50 years ago, but the problem still seems to exist.

Nidds & McGerald (1994) conducted a study of administrators and asked for a list of concerns. Teacher absenteeism and substitute teachers topped the list of concerns. The dilemma was universal, and the frustrations were deep. Yet, when searching educational journals there was extraordinarily little that addressed the problem.

Shaw (1998) a substitute teacher for five years, argues that teachers should have a folder for substitute teachers which would make for a smooth transition into the classroom. She also states substitute teachers should not be responsible for extra duties that a teacher may be responsible for before school to allow the substitute teacher adequate time to go over lessons for the day. However, when reassignment of teacher responsibility is not possible the administrator should supply detailed instructions of the responsibility.

Warner (2003) a substitute teacher and freelance writer expresses his training experience as a substitute teacher. After being fingerprinted and having a background check done, he was shown a video on spilled bodily fluid and taken to a classroom with awaiting students. How scary is that? Warner, 2003 speaks directly to the ineffectiveness of training for substitute teachers from the perspective of a substitute teacher.

In training substitute teachers there are no easy fixes. Substitute teachers have stated that more is needed in classroom management skills (Ezarik, 2004). Classroom management is a difficult concept to teach. Lynch (As cited in Ezarik, 2004), states that some teachers with 20 years experience still encounter problems with classroom management. Since 1995 several districts have called on STI/USU to help with training substitute teachers. Some districts charge participants a $30 to $50 fee to participate in the training. Once training is completed substitute teachers are compensated for participation. In some district's unions have bargained to have training for substitute teachers in their contracts.

In the training sessions for the Wisconsin Education Association Council (WEAC) substitute teachers are trained in the areas of protecting themselves from blood-borne pathogens, and creating lessons plans when in a long-term position (Jehlen, 2004).

Shepherd (1997) states that the Community Schools of Frankfort, in Frankfort Indiana implemented a substitute teacher program. In which all potential substitute teachers must attend the two-hour workshop to work in their district. During the two hours the following are covered: 1) School expectations of substitute teachers. 2) Instructional techniques and classroom control, and 3) A question and answer period.

Sixteen districts in the South Suburbs of a large metropolitan city were found and three of the sixteen school districts had training for substitute teachers. Two districts had a one-day workshop that dealt with classroom management; how to handle discipline, emergencies, school policy, and airborne viruses. Another district conducted training for three hours. This was shocking to say the least that substitute teachers in the South Suburbs of a large metropolitan city were receiving little to no training to be in the classroom.

Summary

All the studies discussed in the literature review were relevant to this study they dealt with a variety of areas that would need to be addressed. The hardships of acquiring substitute teachers. Some advantages to using an online service are: Cutting out the middleman, relieving one person of the duty of calling several substitute teachers. Some advantages to using an online system are: It keeps good records, it does not get tired, and it can match up substitute teacher with the right background by searching the database.

The need of substitute teachers being trained has been dealt with. What is missing from the literature is how effective the training is from the substitute teachers' perspective. This was what was intended to be accomplished after this study was conducted.

CHAPTER THREE: METHODOLOGY

Introduction

Based on previous studies conducted a survey research was chosen to investigate the certified substitute teacher program in the suburbs of a large metropolitan area school district. Chapter three details the methodology and reasoning used in this study. The procedures and processes taken to produce the outcomes of the investigation and explains the research question to be answered by surveying certified substitute teachers. The rationale of the selection process, sample selection techniques, methods of data collection, and methods of data analysis are also explained.

Design

McMillan & Schumacher (2001) states that research methods have a purpose and are systematically chosen to yield data for a problem. The design chosen was done so to yield information geared to the research question. When looking at the topic: An investigation of certified substitute teacher training: What they say is need to be effective in the classroom, there was very little literature from the perspective of the substitute teacher, which lead the researcher to create a survey for substitute teachers to obtain their perspective on training and what they believe to be of importance. The focus of this study was to determine if the training given by the school district was effective for the substitute teacher as it relates to effectiveness in the classroom. In using a mixed method with a quantitative survey research design a written questionnaire was used to gather he

34

information and compile the quantitative data.

Population and Sample

The population for this study was the certified substitute teachers at a suburban school district in a large metropolitan area who had gone through the districts substitute teacher's orientation program. There are approximately 100 substitute teachers employed by the district. All substitute teachers in the state of Illinois must have a four-year bachelor's degree in any field and be state certified to be a substitute teacher. Leedy & Ormrod (2005) said a sample should be selected carefully to ensure the characteristics of the total population are represented, and the results will be exemplary of the total population. The basic rule is the larger the sample size the better. The sample should be able to provide adequate information to generate the outcomes of the study. For population of 100 or less the entire population should be used in the sample. For a population of 500; 50% should be sampled. For 1,500 a sample of 20% should be used. For anything larger than 5,000 a percentage is irrelevant and about 400 for a sample should be sufficient (Leedy & Ormrod 2005). The substitute teachers were the most likely candidates to supply this study with pertinent information as to what substitute teachers say is needed to be more effective in the classroom (McMillan & Schumacher, 2001).

Setting

The setting for this study was a suburban school district of a large metropolitan area. The school district operates on a regular year-round schedule. There are seven schools in the district: 6 K-6 buildings and one middle school. The student population is approximately 2,600; .6% White, 82.6% Black, 14.9% Hispanic, 1.5% Asian/Pacific Islander, and .4% multiracial ethnic backgrounds. There are 147 teachers: 35.4% White, 61.0% Black, and 2.7% Hispanic. 17.7% of the teachers are males and 82.3% are female. The average number of years worked by teachers in the district is 14.8%. 56.5% of the teachers have bachelor's degrees and 43.5% of the teachers have a master's degree.

Instrumentation

In creating the questionnaire survey all questions had to make sure the information being sought was covered. The University of Sheffield (2009) states there are questions based on background information, experience, sensory, opinions, feelings, and knowledge. Questions asked should be geared toward getting information that will be viable to the study. There are also different formats of questions.

Questioning

Dichotomous questions force the person answering to make a choice (i.e. yes, no). This type of question would be used when a clear opinion is needed. (The University of Sheffield, 2009)

Multiple- choice questions provide several discrete responses and would be used when there is complexity in the range of answers. (The University of Sheffield, 2009)

Ranking order provides choices like multiple-choice questions, but it requires the respondent to rank them by priority. This type of question would be used when there is a range of options. (The University of Sheffield, 2009)

Rating question allows individuals to answer with a degree of sensitivity and differentiation while still permitting the researcher to gather quantitative data. This type of question would be used when seeking respondents' attitude about a situation.

Open- ended questions should be used to collect rich qualitative data to describe the respondent's perception. (The University of Sheffield, 2009)

For the questionnaire survey a Likert scale which allows the respondent a range in which they can answer the question (i.e. 1 = Strongly disagree, 5 = Strongly agree) was used (The University of Sheffield, 2009). The rating scale was developed by Rensis Likert in the 1930's to assess people's attitudes (Leedy & Ormond, 2005). This method was considered more useful when evaluating behaviors, attitude, or of phenomenon such as: "inadequate" to "excellent," or "never to always" (p. 185).

After reviewing the literature questions were developed that would be most likely to get the responses needed from certified substitute teachers as to their needs in training. The questionnaire survey had not been used, and no data was collected using this instrument until January 2011 after approval from the Institutional Review Board (IRB) of Argosy University. The instrument was reviewed by two principals and a college professor for typographical errors, readability, and usability. They were asked to mark anything they felt was unclear or confusing while reading through the questions.

After IRB approval a field pilot test of the instrument was conducted using five participants who were not a part of the actual study. This allowed for fine tuning of the instrument to ensure the results desired were expressed in the questionnaire survey. The questionnaire survey is divided into two parts: Part I, General Demographics, where the participant answered questions about their personal background without revealing their name or any information that would identify them. Part II, 24 questions questionnaire with a Likert scale with ratings from 1-5 as to the importance level of each question to the substitute teachers and one open-ended question at the end of the survey. In education research surveys are frequently used to ascertain the attitudes, beliefs, and opinions of educators, which is why this method was chosen (McMillan & Schumacher, 2001). McMillan & Schumacher, (2001) also says, having the same questions for all subjects ensures anonymity.

The questionnaire survey was designed especially for certified substitute teachers to determine needs in future training. McMillan & Schumacher, (2001) list several standards of adequacy that were followed in creating the substitute teacher questionnaire survey:

1. Clear objectives and purpose

2. Targeted population and sampling procedures provide credible answers to research questions

3. Clearly designed and worded, pilot tested and appropriate characteristics for the sample

4. Assurance of confidentiality

5. Established credibility of the research and bias in responses

6. Return rate and follow-up procedures

7. Possible limitations such as return rate influencing conclusion (pp. 314-315).

A quantitative method allowed for easier summarizing, comparing, and generalizations according to the University of Wisconsin EAU CLAIRE (2009).

Procedures

After narrowing down the research topic it was necessary to find a site where the study would be conducted. Superintendents were contacted by phone and emailed. A phone call was received from a superintendent who expressed regret in not being able to assist in the research project. One superintendent never responded. Permission was granted from a superintendent to conduct the study in their school district; an appointment was set up to meet with the superintendent of schools who introduced the researcher to the Human Resource Director to go over the particulars in assisting with the

39

research study. The procedure for their district was for to be fingerprinted and submit personal contact information. A letter of consent was given from the district office to participate in the study (Appendix D).

The pilot test of the substitute teacher questionnaire survey was administered prior to the administration of the final questionnaire survey to ensure the questions rendered the information needed and to make sure it was readable and understandable to the participants. Once the questionnaire survey had been reviewed and validated that the questions would render the information sought; the questionnaire survey was administered to district certified substitute teachers selected for this study.

The substitute teacher orientation is generally conducted in the Fall of every school year prior to the students returning. The questionnaire survey was administered at an Institute Day late in the Spring of 2011. Due to the Privacy Act the district set up the meeting place and invited the substitute teachers to voluntarily participate in the research study. Upon arriving at the designated meeting place verbal explanation was given to the certified substitute teachers regarding the purpose of the study and explained that their participation was strictly voluntary, and they could choose not to participate without consequences. They were also given the information in writing; in the Informed Consent Form (Appendix C) that would be signed if they decided to participate in the study. The consent letter consisted of the nature of the study, the timeframe of the study, and the rights of the participants and any other information needed about the questionnaire survey.

The questionnaire survey took less than 20 minutes to complete. With a low turnout of certified substitute teachers, the first day; other days were set up to accommodate the schedules of those who were not able to make it the first time. The questionnaire surveys were collected by on the same day and numbered.

To ensure that only certified substitute teachers who had gone through the district training participated the last question in Part I of the Demographic section asks if they have attended the district training, if not they were to stop and return the questionnaire survey, if they had attended they were asked to complete Part II of the questionnaire survey.

The University of Wisconsin EAU CLAIRE (2009) says, in completing questionnaires/surveys people are usually more truthful when the responses are anonymous. Some drawbacks to this method would be getting all the substitute teachers to come in on their own to complete the questionnaire survey.

Questionnaire Survey Data Collection

In the data collection process the surveys were numbered as they were returned. Once all surveys were returned, they were grouped and categorized. The data was then put into a Microsoft spreadsheet and transferred to the Statistical Package for the Social Science (SPSS 15.0) software, the questionnaire surveys were numbered to

41

keep the inputting in order, and to ensure that every questionnaire survey was accounted for and documented especially since the data collection took more than one day to collect. The data was then organized and analyzed using the cross-tabulation functions of SPSS to describe participant demographics and responses given by the participants. The results and conclusions were then presented in tables, and charts based on the percentages calculated from the data. To interpret and analyze the results the data was constructed around the research question, to present the findings.

Summary

Chapter Three discusses in detail the steps taken in the research methodology used for this study in finding out what certified substitute teachers say is needed from the substitute teacher training program to be effective in the classroom. The survey research method was chosen to assess what was being done and how effective it was from the substitute teachers' perspective. A convenient sample of substitute teachers that had gone through the district training program was utilized to complete the questionnaire survey and an open-ended question for the study.

CHAPTER FOUR: FINDINGS AND ANALYSIS

Overview

The purpose of the study was to obtain the perspective of the certified substitute teacher and what they say is needed in training to be effective in the classroom. A certified substitute teacher is one who possesses a bachelor's degree in any field, has obtained certification as a substitute teacher in the state of Illinois, and received a substitute teachers' license.

A mixed methodology research was implemented for this study. The survey instrument, Self-Administered Questionnaire: An Investigation of training Certified Substitute teachers and what They Say is needed to be Effective in the classroom consisted of two parts. Part I detailing the demographics of the participant and Part II a Likert scale questionnaire regarding the importance of needs for the certified substitute teacher in the classroom, and one open-ended question relative to the needs of certified substitute teachers. Five (5) certified substitute teachers served as a pilot test group to determine questionnaire construction, time allotment, readability, and validity of the study. These substitute teachers did not later participate in the population surveyed for the study.

Data Collection Procedures

In working with the Human Resource Director of the school district surveyed in the South Suburbs of Chicago invitations were sent out to certified substitute teachers.

The Human Resource Director helped in setting up two dates for certified substitute teachers to come out and complete the survey. On the first two dates nine (9) certified substitute teachers came out to complete the survey, a flyer also went out to encourage certified substitute teachers to participate in the study. Four more dates were scheduled for the month of May for certified substitute teachers to come out and participate in the study.

Once all dates had passed and surveys were collected the SPSS statistical software was used to conduct a cross tabulation of the survey data collected to ascertain the percentages of participants importance to the survey questions. Afterwards the data was reviewed from SPSS statistical software package and nominal variables were used to disseminate the demographic characteristics. Data from the Likert scale questionnaire (Appendix A) were coded as ordinal variables and transformed to create new variables for comparison purposes.

Population

The population included certified substitute teachers who had gone through the school districts training program. The survey was administered in person in a large conference room to nine (9) participants at two different times. Participants were told why they were there and the purpose and process in which the survey would be administered was explained. One participant felt they did not meet the criteria of the study being a retired teacher working in the district and asked to be dismissed from the

44

conference room.

An opportunity was given to seventy-five (75) certified substitute teachers that worked in the district being studied, nine (9) or 12% responded and eight (8) or 11% completed the survey. Unfortunately, 66 or (89%) of the certified substitute teacher pool in this South Suburban School District chose not to respond.

The Instrument

The Self-Administered Questionnaire Survey: An Investigation of Training Certified Substitute Teachers and What They Say Is Needed to Be Effective in the Classroom was designed as a mixed questionnaire (Henderson, 2011), in which both quantitative and qualitative data were collected simultaneously (Appendix A). The survey consisted of two parts: Demographic information and a twenty-four (24) question questionnaire on the importance of training with a Likert scale ranging from 1-5, and an open-ended question regarding other needs as seen by the certified substitute teacher. The open-ended question used was to gain more insight into what the certified substitute teachers thought. It allowed the substitute teacher to elaborate on what they felt was needed. The responses to the open-ended questions were useful; responses gave information not gathered from the questionnaire. Rich, thick descriptions of the phenomena were revealed about the study.

The survey developed collected data that determined the needs of certified substitute teachers in training programs from their perspective and established what certified substitute teachers say is needed to be effective in the classroom. Twenty-four (24) questions dealt with what certified substitute teachers deemed to be important in training. Respondents were also asked to respond to the following open-ended question: "Please add any comments below you believe will be helpful in knowing what substitutes feel is needed in training to be effective in the classroom".

Results of the Analysis

Demographic Respondents

Responses in the analysis are based on the certified substitute teachers who completed the school districts training program. As stated, prior, nine (9) respondents represented a 12% response rate. Consequently, eight (8) completed the survey which gives a response rate of 11%. The demographic characteristics are displayed in Table 1. Responses not answered or skipped were counted as missing data. The data revealed most of the respondents were female 5 or 62.5% and 3 or 37.5% of the respondents were males. One certified substitute teacher or 12.5% of the respondents taught grades 3-5 while 7 or 87.5% taught all grades, all being (K-8). Black/African Americans made up most respondents for this study with 7 or 87.5% and 1or 12.5% of the respondents were White. 2 or 25% of the certified substitute teachers were day to day substitutes. (4) 50% were substitute teachers in all areas (i.e. day to day, floater, long term, short call, or permanent). 1 or 12.5% had been a day to day substitute teacher and a floater and the other 1 or 12.5% had been a day to day substitute teacher and a permanent

substitute teacher in the district. 8 or 100% of the respondents had gone through the

district training program. 6 or 75% of the respondents' only substitute taught in the

district studied, however, 2 or 25% of the respondents were substitute teachers in other

districts. 3 or 37.5% of the respondents had been a substitute teacher for 1-3 years. 1 or

12.5% had been a substitute teacher for 3-5 year. 2 or 25% had been a substitute teacher

for 7-10 years and 2 or 25% had been a substitute teacher for 10 or more years.

Table 1: Demographic Characteristics of Respondents in the Study

Demographics		N	%
Gender			
	Male	3	37.5%
	Female	5	62.5%
Grades Taught			
	3-5	1	12.5%
	K-8	7	87.5%
Race			
	Black/African-American	7	87.5%
	White	1	12.5%
Type of Substituting			
	Day to day	2	25%
	All Areas	4	50%
	Day to day/floater	1	12.5%
	Day to day/permanent	1	12.5%

Training			
	District Training	8	100%
Substitute Pool			
	Only this district	6	75%
	Other districts	2	25%
Years Substituting			
	1-3 years	3	37.5%
	3-5 years	1	12.5%
	7-10 years	2	25%
	10 or more years	2	25%

Categories of Importance

The study was an investigation to what certified substitute teachers say is needed to be effective in the classroom through training. The following section reports the results of the data collected from the surveys. Four categories were identified and coded from the questions on the survey: Building Procedures (BP), Training (TR), Classroom Management (CM), and Classroom Procedures (CP). Percentages of importance were derived from the responses for each question as it related to the categories derived from the coding of the survey and the demographics of the participants. The letter Q and the corresponding numbers were used to represent the questions from the survey.

Building Procedures

Nine (9) questions on the survey were coded under building procedures; Q1, Q2, Q3, Q4, Q14, Q15, Q17, Q19 and Q24. Using SPSS statistical software package, responses were examined and compared with the importance of each question based on the rating give by the respondent. Rank scores used for the survey were:

1=not important 2=least important 3=somewhat important 4= important 5= especially important.

The information was cross tabulated with gender, race, grades taught, years of experience, type of substituting, and training.

Table 2 shows the responses for both genders and the percentages of importance for each question.

Gender

Q1 – Attending building meetings 1 or 12.5% of males said this was least important, somewhat important, and important. While 4 or 50% of females said this is important and 1 or 12.5% of females said this is least important.

Q2 – Attending District in-services 1 or 12.5% of males said this was somewhat important and 2 or 25% of males said this is important 1 or 12.5% of females said this is least important. 3 or 37.5% said this is important, and 1 or 12.5% of females said this is especially important.

Q3 – Administrative supervision 1 or 12.5% of males said this is not important, least important, and somewhat important. While 2 or 25% of females said this is not important and important another 1 or 12.5% said this is somewhat important.

Q4- Written or verbal feedback 1 or 12.5% of males said this is somewhat important, while 2 or 25% of males said this is important. 1 or 12.5% of females said this is not important, while 2 or 25% said this is somewhat important and important.

Q14- Understanding the bell schedule 2 or 25% of males said this is important while 1 or 12.5% said this is especially important. 1 or 12.5% of females said this is somewhat important and important, while 3 or 37.5% said this is especially important.

Q15- Understanding the master bell schedule 1 or 12.5% of males said this is somewhat important and 2 or 25% said this is important. 1 or 12.5% of females said this is least important, somewhat important, and important, while 2 or 25% of females said this is especially important.

Q17- Feel like a part of the staff 2 or 25% of males said this is important and 1 or 12.5% said this is especially important. 1 or 12.5% of females said this is least important while 2 or 25% said this is important and especially important.

Q19- Knowing building procedures 1 or 12.5% of males said this is important while 2 or 25% said this is especially important. 1 or 12.5% of females said this is important, while 4 or 50% said this is especially important.

Q24- Having an I.D 1 or 12.5% of males said this is least important and 2 or 25% said this is somewhat important. 1 or 12.5% of females said this is not important, somewhat important, and especially important, while 2 or 25% said this is especially important.

Table 2 – (BP)/Gender - Importance

Question	Gender	Not important	Least important	Somewhat important	Important	Especially important
Q1- Attending building meetings.	Male		(1) 12.5%	(1) 12.5%	(1) 12.5%	
	Female		(1) 12.5%		(4) 50%	
Q2 – Attending district in-services.	Male			(1) 12.5%	(2) 25%	
	Female		(1) 12.5%		(3)37.5%	(1)12.5%
Q3- Administrative supervision.	Male	(1)12.5%	(1)12.5%	(1)12.5%		
	Female	(2)25%		(1)12.5%	(2)25%	
Q4-Written or verbal feedback.	Male			(1)12.5%	(2)25%	
	Female	(1)12.5%		(2)25%	(2)25%	
Q14- Bell schedule	Male				(2)25%	(1)12.5%
	Female			(1)12.5%	(1)12.5%	(3)37.5%
Q15- Master bell schedule	Male			(1)12.5%	(2)25%	
	Female		(1)12.5%	(1)12.5%	(1)12.5%	(2)25%
Q17- Feeling like a part of the staff.	Male				(2)25%	(1)12.5%
	Female		(1)12.5%		(2)25%	(2)25%
Q19- Appropriate BP	Male				(1)12.5%	(2)25%
	Female				(1)12.5%	(4)50%
Q24- Having an I.D.	Male		(1)12.5%	(2)25%		
	Female	(1)12.5%		(1)12.5%	(2)25%	(1)12.5%

Overall, there were several building procedures that are important to male and female certified substitute teachers. The responses identified what they felt would be important in training for their effectiveness in the classroom. Attending building meetings, districts in-services, understanding the bell schedule and master bell schedule, feeling like a part of the staff and knowing appropriate building procedures are at the top of the list for both genders.

Table 2.1 shows the responses for both races and the percentages of importance for each question.

Race

Q1- Attending building meetings 1 or 12.5% of African Americans said this is least important and somewhat important, while 5 or 62.5% of said this is important. 1 or 12.5% of Whites said this is least important.

Q2 – Attending District in-services 1 or 12.5% of African Americans said this is somewhat important, 5 or 62.5% said this is important, and 1 or 12.5% said this is especially important. 1 or 12.5% of Whites said this is least important.

Q3- Administrative supervision 2 or 25% of African Americans said this is not important, somewhat important, and important while 1 or 12.5% said this is least important. 1 or 12.5% of Whites said this is not important.

Q4 – Written or verbal feedback 1 or 12.5% of African Americans said this is not important while 2 or 25% said this is somewhat important and 4 or 50% said this is important. 1 or 12.5% of Whites said this is somewhat important.

Q14 – Understanding the bell schedule 1 or 12.5% of African Americans said this is somewhat important. 3 or 37.5% said this is important and especially important. 1 or

12.5% of Whites said this is especially important.

Q15 – Understanding the master bell schedule 1 or 12.5% of African Americans said this is least important and especially important. 2 or 25% said this is somewhat important and 3 or 37.5% said this is important. 1 or 12.5% of Whites said this is especially important.

Q17 – Feel like a part of the staff 1 or 12.5% of African Americans said this is least important, 4 or 50% said this is important, and 2 or 25% said this is especially important. 1 or 12.5% of Whites said this is especially important.

Q19 – Knowing building procedures 2 or 25% of African Americans said this is important. 5 or 62.5% of African Americans said this is especially important. 1 or 12.5% of Whites said this is especially important.

Q24 – Having an I.D. 1 or 12.5% of African Americans said this is not important, least important, and especially important. While 2 or 25% of African Americans said this is somewhat important and important. 1 or 12.5% of Whites said this somewhat important.

Table 2.1 – (BP)/Race - Importance

Question	Race	Not important	Least important	Somewhat important	Important	Especially important
Q1- Attending building meetings.	African American	(1)12.5%		(1)12.5%	(5)62.5%	
	White		(1)12.5%			
Q2 – Attending district in-services.	African American			(1)12.5%	(5)62.5%	(1)12.5%
	White		(1)12.5%			
Q3- Administrative supervision.	African American	(2)25%	(1)12.5%	(2)25%	(2)25%	
	White	(1)12.5%				
Q4-Written or verbal feedback.	African American	(1)12.5%		(2)25%	(4)50%	
	White			(1)12.5%		
Q14- Bell schedule	African American			(1)12.5%	(3)37.5%	(3)37.5%
	White					(1)12.5%
Q15- Master bell schedule	African American		(1)12.5%	(2)25%	(3)37.5%	(1)12.5%
	White					(1)12.5%
Q17- Feeling like a part of the staff.	African American		(1)12.5%		(4)50%	(2)25%
	White					(1)12.5%
Q19- Appropriate BP	African American				(2)25%	(5)62.5%
	White					(1)12.5%
Q24- Having an I.D.	African American	(1)12.5%	(1)12.5%	(2)25%	(2)25%	(1)12.5%
	White				(1)12.5%	

Overall, there were several building procedures that are important to African American's as well as White certified substitute teachers. The responses identified what they felt would be helpful in training for their effectiveness in the classroom. Attending building meetings, districts in-services, written or verbal feedback, understanding the bell schedule and master bell schedule, feeling like a part of the staff, and knowing appropriate building procedures are at the top of the list for both races.

Table 2.2 shows the responses for the grades taught and the percentages of importance for each question.

Grades Taught

Q1 – Attending building meetings 1 or 12.5% of certified substitute teachers who taught grades 3-5 said this is important. 2 or 25% who taught K-8 said this is least important. 1 or 12.5% said this is somewhat important and 4 or 50% said this is important.

Q2 – Attending district in-services 1 or 12.5% of certified substitute teachers who taught grades 3-5 said this is especially important. 1 or 12.5% who taught K-8 said this is least important and somewhat important, while 5 or 62.5% said this is important.

Q3 – Administrative supervision 1 or 12.5% of certified substitute teachers who taught grades 3-5 said this is not important. 2 or 25% who taught grades K-8 said this is not important, somewhat important, and important and 1 or 12.5% said this is least important.

Q4 – Written or verbal feedback 1 or 12.5% of certified substitute teachers who taught grades 3-5 said this is not important. 3 or 37.5% who taught K-8 said this is somewhat important, while 4 or 50% said this is important.

Q14 – Understanding the bell schedule 1 or 12.5% of certified substitute teachers who taught grades 3-5 said this is especially important. 1 or 12.5% who taught K-8 said this is somewhat important. 3 or 37.5% said this is important and especially important.

Q15 – Understanding the master bell schedule 1 or 12.5% of certified substitute teachers who taught grades 3-5 said this is least important. 2 or 25% who taught grades K-8 said this is somewhat important and especially important, while 3 or 37.5% said this is important.

Q17 – Feel like a part of the staff 1 or 12.5% of certified substitute teachers who taught grades 3-5 said this is least important. 4 or 50% who taught K-8 said this is important and 3 or 37.5% said this is especially important.

Q19 – Knowing building procedures 1 or 12.5% of certified substitute teachers who taught grades 3-5 said this is especially important. 2 or 25% who taught grades K-8 said this is important and 2 or 25% said this is especially important.

Q24 – Having an I.D. 1 or 12.5% of certified substitute teachers who taught grades 3-5 said this is not important. 1 or 12.5% who taught grades K-8 said this is least important and especially important. 3 or 37.5% said this is somewhat important and 2 or 25% said this is important.

Table 2.2 – (BP)/Grades Taught- Importance

Question	Grades taught	Not important	Least important	Somewhat important	Important	Especially important
Q1- Attending building meetings.	3-5				(1)12.5%	
	K-8		(2)25%	(1)12.5%	(4)50%	
Q2 – Attending district in-services.	3-5				(1)12.5%	
	K-8		(1)12.5%	(1)12.5%	(5)62.5%	
Q3- Administrative supervision.	3-5	(1)12.5%				
	K-8	(2)25%	(1)12.5%	(2)25%	(2)25%	
Q4-Written or verbal feedback.	3-5	(1)12.5%				
	K-8			(3)37.5%	(4)50%	
Q14- Bell schedule	3-5				(1)12.5%	
	K-8			(1)12.5%	(3)37.5%	(3)37.5%
Q15- Master bell schedule	3-5		(1)12.5%			
	K-8			(2)25%	(3)37.5%	(2)25%
Q17- Feeling like a part of the staff.	3-5		(1)12.5%			
	K-8				(4)50%	(3)37.5%
Q19- Appropriate BP	3-5					(1)12.5%
	K-8				(2)25%	(5)62.5%
Q24- Having an I.D.	3-5	(1)12.5%				
	K-8		(1)12.5%	(3)37.5%	(2)25%	(1)12.5%

Overall, there were several building procedures that are important to certified substitute teachers that teach grades 3-5 and K-8. The responses identified what certified substitutes say would be important in training for their effectiveness in the classroom. Again, attending building meetings, districts in-services, written or verbal feedback, understanding the bell schedule and master bell schedule, feeling like a part of the staff, and knowing appropriate building procedures are at the top of the list for grades taught, especially those teaching in grades K-8.

Table 2.3 shows the responses for the years of substituting and the percentages of importance for each question.

Years of Substituting

Q1 – Attending building meetings 2 or 25% of certified substitute teachers who have taught for 1-3 years said this is least important and 1 or 12.5% said this is important. 1 or 12.5% who taught 3-5 years said this is important. 1 or 12.5% who taught 7-10 years said this is somewhat important and important. 2 or 25% who taught 10 or more years said this is important.

Q2 – Attending district in-services 1 or 12.5% of certified substitute teachers who taught 1-3 years said this is least important and 2 or 25% said this is important. 1 or 12.5% who taught 3-5 years said this is important. 1 or 12.5% teaching 7-10 years said this is somewhat important and especially important. 2 or 25% who taught 10 or more years said this is important.

Q3 – Administrative supervision 2 or 25% of certified substitute teachers who taught 1-3 years said this is not important. 1 or 12.5% said this is least important. 1 or 12.5% teaching 3-5 years said this is important. 1 or 12.5% teaching 7-10 years said this is not important and somewhat important. 1 or 12.5% teaching 10 or more years said this is somewhat important and important.

Q4- Written and verbal feedback 2 or 25% teaching 1-3 years said this is somewhat important and important. 1 or 12.5% teaching 3-5 years said this is somewhat important and important. 1 or 12.5% teaching 7-10 years said this is not important and important. 1 or 12.5% teaching 10 or more years said this is somewhat important and important.

Q14 - Understanding the bell schedule 1 or 12.5% of certified substitute teachers who taught 1-3 years said this is important and 2 or 25% said this is especially important. 1 or 12.5% teaching 3-5 years said this is somewhat important. 1 or 12.5% teaching 7-10 years said this is important and especially important. 1 or 12.5% teaching 10 or more years said this is important and especially important.

Q15 – Understanding the master bell schedule 1 or 12.5% of certified substitute teachers who taught 1-3 years said this is somewhat important, important, and especially important. 1 or 12.5% teaching 3-5 years said this is somewhat important. 1 or 12.5% teaching 7-10 years said this is least important and important. 1 or 12.5% teaching 10 or more years said this is important and especially important.

Q17 – Feel like a part of the staff 1 or 12.5% of certified substitute teachers who taught

1-3 years said this is important and 2 or 25% said this is especially important. 1 or 12.5% teaching 3-5 years said this is especially important. 1 or 12.5% teaching 7-10 years said this is least important and important. 2 or 25% teaching 10 or more years said this is important.

Q19 – Knowing building procedures 1 or 12.5% of certified substitute teachers who taught 1-3 years said this is important and especially important. 2 or 25% said this is especially important. 1 or 12.5% teaching 3-5 years said this is important. 2 or 25% of teaching 7-10 years said this is especially important. 2 or 25% teaching 10 or more years said this is especially important.

Q24 – Having an I.D. 1 or 12.5% of certified substitute teachers who taught 1-3 years said this is least important. 2 or 25% said this is somewhat important. 1 or 12.5% teaching 3-5 years said this is important. 1 or 12.5% teaching 7-10 years said this is least important and somewhat important. 1 or 12.5% teaching 10 or more years said this is important and especially important.

Table 2.3 – (BP)/Years of Substituting- Importance

Question	Years of Substituting	Not important	Least important	Somewhat important	Important	Especially important
Q1- Attending building meetings.	1-3 years		(2)25%		(1)12.5%	
	3-5 years				(1)12.5%	
	7-10 years			(1)12.5%	(1)12.5%	
	10 or more years					(2)25%
Q2 – Attending district in-services.	1-3 years		(1)12.5%		(2)25%	
	3-5 years				(1)12.5%	
	7-10 years			(1)12.5%		(1)12.5%
	10 or more years					(2)25%
Q3- Administrative supervision.	1-3 years	(2)25%	(1)12.5%			
	3-5 years				(1)12.5%	
	7-10 years	(1)12.5%		(1)12.5%		
	10 or more years			(1)12.5%		(1)12.5%
Q4-Written or verbal feedback.	1-3 years			(2)25%	(2)25%	
	3-5 years			(1)12.5%	(1)12.5%	
	7-10 years	(1)12.5%			(1)12.5%	
	10 or more years			(1)12.5%	(1)12.5%	
Q14- Bell schedule	1-3 years				(1)12.5%	(2)25%
	3-5 years			(1)12.5%		
	7-10 years				(1)12.5%	(1)12.5%
	10 or more years				(1)12.5%	(1)12.5%
Q15- Master bell schedule	1-3 years			(1)12.5%	(1)12.5%	(1)12.5%
	3-5 years			(1)12.5%		
	7-10 years		(1)12.5%		(1)12.5%	
	10 or more years				(1)12.5%	(1)12.5%
Q17- Feeling like a part of the staff.	1-3 years				(1)12.5%	(2)25%
	3-5 years					(1)12.5%
	7-10 years		(1)12.5%			(1)12.5%

	10 or more years				(2)25%	
Q19- Appropriate BP	1-3 years				(1)12.5%	(2)25%
	3-5 years				(1)12.5%	
	7-10 years					(2)25%
	10 or more years					(2)25%
Q24- Having an I.D.	1-3 years		(1)12.5%	(2)25%		
	3-5 years				(1)12.5%	
	7-10 years		(1)12.5%	(1)12.5%		
	10 or more years				(1)12.5%	(1)12.5%

Overall, there were several building procedures that are important to certified substitute teachers who just started substitute teaching and for those who have been substitute teaching for many years. The responses identified what certified substitute teachers say would be important in training for their effectiveness in the classroom. Again, attending building meetings, districts in-services, written or verbal feedback, understanding the bell schedule and master bell schedule, feeling like a part of the staff, and knowing appropriate building procedures were at the top of the list for all substitutes regardless of how long they had been substituting.

Table 2.4 shows the responses for the different types of substituting and the percentages of importance for each question.

Type of Substituting

Q1 – Attending building meetings 1 or 12.5% of certified substitute teachers teaching day to day said this is least important and 1 or 12.5% said this is important. 4 or 50% of substitute teachers in all areas said this is important. 1 or 12.5% of day to day and floater substitute teachers said this is least important. 1 or 12.5% of day to day and permanent substitute teacher said this is somewhat important.

Q2 – Attending district in-services 2 or 25% of day to day substitute teachers said this is important. 3 or 37.5% of all substitute teachers said this is important and 1 or 12.5% said this is especially important. 1 or 12.5% of day to day and floater substitute teachers said this is least important. 1 or 12.5% of day to day and permanent substitute teacher said this is somewhat important.

Q3 – Administrative supervision 1 or 12.5% of day to day substitute teachers said this is not important and least important. 1 or 12.5% of all substitute teachers said this is not important and somewhat important. 1 or 12.5% of day to day and floater substitute teachers said this is not important. 1 or 12.5% of day to day and permanent substitute teachers said this is somewhat important.

Q4 – Written or verbal feedback 1 or 12.5% of day to day substitute teachers said this is somewhat important and important. 1 or 12.5% of all substitute teachers said this is not important and somewhat important. 2 or 25% said this is important. 1 or 12.5% of day to day and floater substitute teachers said this is somewhat important. 1 or 12.5% of day to day and permanent substitute teachers said this is important.

Q14 – Understanding the bell schedule 1 or 12.5% of day to day substitute teachers said this is important and especially important. 1 or 12.5% of all substitute teachers said this is somewhat important and important and 2 or 25% said this is especially important. 1 or 12.5% of day to day and floater substitute teachers said this is especially important. 1 or 12.5% day to day and permanent substitute teachers said this is important.

Q15 – Understanding the master bell schedule 1 or 12.5% of day to day substitute teachers said this is somewhat important and important. 1 or 12.5% of all substitute teachers said this is least important, somewhat important, important, and especially important. 1 or 12.5% of day to day and floater substitute teachers said this is especially important. 1 or 12.5% of day to day and permanent substitute teachers said this is important.

Q17 – Feel like a part of the staff 1 or 12.5% of day to day substitute teachers said this is important and especially important. 1 or 12.5% of all substitute teachers said this is least important and especially important and 2 or 25% said it is important. 1 or 12.5% of day to day and floater substitute teachers said this is especially important and 1 or 12.5% of day to day and permanent substitute teachers said this is important.

Q19 – Knowing building procedures 1 or 12.5% of day to day substitute teachers said this is important and especially important. 1 or 12.5% of all substitute teachers said this is important and 3 or 37.5% said this is especially important. 1 or 12.5% of day to day and floater substitute teachers said this is especially important. 1 or 12.5% of day to day and permanent substitute teachers said this is especially important.

Q24 – Having an I.D. 1 or 12.5% day today substitute teachers said this is least important and somewhat important. 1 or 12.5% of all substitute teachers said this is not important and especially important and 2 or 25% said this is important. 1 or 12.5% of day to day and floater substitute teachers said this is somewhat important. 1 or 12.5% of day to day and permanent substitute teachers said this is somewhat important.

Table 2.4 – (BP)/Types of Substituting- Importance

Question	Type of Substituting	Not important	Least important	Somewhat important	Important	Especially important
Q1- Attending building meetings.	Day to day		(1)12.5%		(1)12.5%	
	All				(4)50%	
	Day to day/floater		(1)12.5%			
	Day to day/permanent			(1)12.5%		
Q2 – Attending district in-services.	Day to day				(2)25%	
	All				(3)37.5%	(1)12.5%
	Day to day/floater		(1)12.5%			
	Day to day/permanent			(1)12.5%		
Q3- Administrative supervision.	Day to day	(1)12.5%	(1)12.5%			
	All	(1)12.5%		(1)12.5%		
	Day to day/floater		(1)12.5%			
	Day to day/permanent			(1)12.5%		
Q4-Written or verbal feedback.	Day to day			(1)12.5%	(1)12.5%	
	All	(1)12.5%		(1)12.5%	(2)25%	
	Day to day/floater			(1)12.5%		
	Day to day/permanent				(1)12.5%	
Q14- Bell schedule	Day to day				(1)12.5%	(1)12.5%
	All			(1)12.5%	(1)12.5%	(2)25%
	Day to day/floater					(1)12.5%
	Day to day/permanent				(1)12.5%	
Q15- Master bell schedule	Day to day			(1)12.5%	(1)12.5%	

Question	Type					
	All		(1)12.5%	(1)12.5%	(1)12.5%	(1)12.5%
	Day to day/floater					
	Day to day/permanent				(1)12.5%	(1)12.5%
Q17- Feeling like a part of the staff.	Day to day				(1)12.5%	(1)12.5%
	All		(1)12.5%		(2)25%	(1)12.5%
	Day to day/floater					
	Day to day/permanent				(1)12.5%	(1)12.5%
Q19- Appropriate BP	Day to day				(1)12.5%	(1)12.5%
	All				(1)12.5%	(3)37.5%
	Day to day/floater					
	Day to day/permanent				(1)12.5%	(1)12.5%
Q24- Having an I.D.	Day to day		(1)12.5%	(1)12.5%		
	All	(1)12.5%			(2)25%	(1)12.5%
	Day to day/floater					
	Day to day/permanent			(1)12.5%		
				(1)12.5%		

Overall, there were several building procedures that are important to certified substitute teachers regardless of the type of substituting assignment. The responses identified what they say would be important in training for their effectiveness in the classroom. Again, attending building meetings, districts in-services, written or verbal feedback, understanding the bell schedule and master bell schedule, feeling like a part of the staff, and knowing appropriate building procedures are at the top of the list for all types of substitutes.

Table 2.5 shows the responses for the certified substitute teachers that have gone through the district training program and the percentages of importance for each question.

Trained Substitutes

Q1 – Attending building meetings 1 or 25% said this is least important, 1 or 12.5% said this is somewhat important and 5 or 62.5% said this is important.

Q2 – Attending district in-services 1 or 12.5% said this is least important, somewhat important, and especially important, while 5 or 62.5% said this is important.

Q3 – Administrative supervision 3 or 37.5% said this is not important. 1 or 12.5% said this is least important. 2 or 25% said this is somewhat important and important.

Q4 – Written or verbal feedback 1 or 12.5% said this is not important. 3 or 37.5% said this is somewhat important and 4 or 50% said this is important.

Q14 – Understanding the bell schedule 1 or 12.5% said this is somewhat important 3 or 37.5% said this is important and 4 or 50% said this is especially important.

Q15 – Understanding the master bell schedule 1 or 12.5% said this is least important. 2 or 25% said this is somewhat important, 3 or 37.5% said this is important and 2 or 25% said this is especially important.

Q17 – feel like a part of the staff 1 or 12.5% said this is least important. 4 or 50% said this is important, and 3 or 37.5% said this is especially important.

Q19 – Knowing building procedures 2 or 25% said this is important and 6 or 75% said this is especially important.

Q24 – Having an I. D. 1 or 12.5% said this is not important, least important, and

especially important. 3 or 37.5% said this is somewhat important and 2 or 25% said this

is important.

Table 2.5 – (BP)/Trained Substitutes- Importance

Question	Trained Substitutes	Not important	Least important	Somewhat important	Important	Especially important
Q1- Attending building meetings.			(2)25%	(1)12.5%	(5)62.5%	
Q2 – Attending district in-services.			(1)12.5%	(1)12.5%	(5)62.5%	(1)12.5%
Q3- Administrative supervision.		(3)37.5%	(1)12.5%	(2) 25%	(2)25%	
Q4-Written or verbal feedback.		(1)12.5%		(3)37.5%	(4)50%	
Q14- Bell schedule				(1)12.5%	(3)37.5%	(4) 50%
Q15- Master bell schedule			(1)12.5%	(2)25%	(3)37.5%	(2)25%
Q17- Feeling like a part of the staff.		(1)12.5%			(4)50%	(3)37.5%
Q19- Appropriate BP					(2)25%	(6)75%
Q24- Having an I.D.		(1)12.5%	(1)12.5%		(2) 25%	(1)12.5%

Overall, despite previous training there were several building procedures that are

important to certified substitute teachers. The responses identified what certified

substitute teachers say would be important in training for their effectiveness in the

68

classroom. Again, attending building meetings, districts in-services, written or verbal feedback, understanding the bell schedule and master bell schedule, feeling like a part of the staff, and knowing appropriate building procedures are at the top of the list for all types of substitutes.

Training

Seven questions on the survey were coded under the category of training. Q5, Q6, Q7, Q9, Q10, Q16, and Q18. Using SPSS statistical software package, responses were examined and compared with the importance of each question based on the rating give by the respondent. Rank scores used for the survey were:

1=not important 2=least important 3=somewhat important 4= important 5= especially important.

Table 3 shows the response from the certified substitute teacher based on both genders and the percentages of importance for each question.

Gender

Q5 - When asked about training on writing a classroom management plan 1 or 12.5% of males said this is least important, somewhat important and important. 1 or 12.5% of females said this is least important and somewhat important. While 3 or 37.5% said this is important.

Q6 – When asked about training on how to handle disruptive students 1 or 14.3% of males said this is least important and 2 or 28.6% said this is especially important. 1 or 14.3% of females said this is important and 3 or 42.9% said this is especially important. All respondents did not answer this question.

Q7 – When asked about training on how to determine the difference between major and minor infractions 1 or 12.5% of males said this is not important, least important, and important. 1 or 12.5% of females said this is least important, somewhat important, and important. 2 or 25% said this is especially important.

Q9 – When asked about having training on how to plan a basic lesson 1 or 12.5% of males said this is not important, important, and especially important. 1 or 12.5% of females said this is not important, somewhat important, and especially important, 2 or 25% said this is important

Q10 – When asked about training on how to deliver instruction 1 or 16.7% of males said this is not important. 2 or 33.3% said this is important. 2 or 33.3% of females said this is somewhat important and 1 or 16.7% said this is important. All respondents did not answer this question.

Q16 – When asked about having training more than once a year 1 or 14.3% of males said this is least important, somewhat important, and especially important, 2 or 28.6% of females said this is important and especially important. All respondents did not answer this question.

Q18 – When asked about giving input on training for in-services 2 or 25% of males said this is somewhat important and 1 or 12.5% said this is especially important. 1 or 12.5% of females said this is least important, somewhat important, and important. 2 or 25% said this is especially important.

Table 3 – (TR)/Gender - Importance

Question	Gender	Not important	Least important	Somewhat important	Important	Especially important
Q5 – Classroom management plan	Male		(1)12.5%	(1)12.5%	(1)12.5%	
	Female		(1)12.5%	(1)12.5%	(3)37.5%	
Q6 – Handling disruptive students	Male		(1)14.3%			(2)26.6%
	Female				(1)14.3%	(3)42.9%
Q7 – Difference between major/minor infractions	Male	(1)12.5%	(1)12.5%		(1)12.5%	
	Female		(1)12.5%	(1)12.5%	(1)12.5%	(2)25%
Q9 – Plan a basic lesson	Male	(1)12.5%			(1)12.5%	(1)12.5%
	Female	(1)12.5%		(1)12.5%	(2)25%	(1)12.5%
Q10 – Delivery of instruction	Male	(1)16.7%			(2)33.3%	
	Female			(2)33.3%	(1)16.7%	
Q16 – More than one training session per…	Male		(1)14.3%	(1)14.3%		(1)14.3%
	Female				(2)28.6%	(2)28.6%
Q18- Giving input on in-services	Male			(2) 25%		(1)12.5%
	Female		(1)12.5%	(1)12.5%	(1)12.5%	(2)25%

Overall, despite previous training there were several areas in training that are important to certified substitute teachers. The responses identified what certified substitute teachers say would be important in training for their effectiveness in the classroom. The areas identified as being of importance in training are writing a classroom management plan, how to handle disruptive students, the difference between a major/minor infraction, planning a basic lesson, how to deliver instruction, having more than one training per year, and giving input for training in-services. Even though all questions are of concern, handling disruptive students and more than one training session per year held the largest percentages of importance.

Table 3.1 shows the response from the certified substitute teacher based on both races and the percentages of importance for each question.

Race

Q5 – When asked about training on writing a classroom management plan 1 or 12.5% of African Americans said this is least important. 2 or 25% said this is somewhat important and 4 or 50% said this is important. 1 or 12.5% of Whites said this is least important.

Q6 – When asked about training on how to handle disruptive students 1 or 14.3% of African Americans said this is least important and important. 4 or 57.1% said this is especially important. 1 or 14.3% of Whites said this is especially important. All respondents did not answer this question.

Q7 – When asked about training on how to determine the difference between major and minor infractions 1 or 12.5% of African Americans said this is not important, somewhat important, and especially important. 2 or 25% said this is least important and important. 1 or 12.5% of Whites said this is especially important.

Q9 – When asked about having training on how to plan a basic lesson 1 or 12.5% of African Americans said this is not important and somewhat important. 3 or 37.5% said this is important and 2 or 25% said this is especially important. 1 or 12.5% of Whites said this is not important.

Q10 – When asked about training on how to deliver instruction 1 or 16.7% of African Americans said this is not important and somewhat important. 1 or 16.7% of Whites said this is somewhat important.

Q16 – When asked about having training more than once a year 1 or 14.3% of African American said this is least important, somewhat important, and especially important while 3 or 50% said this is important. 1 or 14.3% of Whites said this is especially important. All respondents did not answer this question.

Q18 – When asked about giving input on training for in-services 1 or 12.5% of African Americans said this is least important and important. 3 or 37.5% said this is somewhat important and 2 or 25% said this is especially important. 1 or 12.5% of Whites said this is especially important.

Table 3.1 – (TR)/Race - Importance

Question	Race	Not important	Least important	Somewhat important	Important	Especially important
Q5 – Classroom management plan	African American	(1)12.5%		(2) 25%	(4)50%	
	White		(1)12.5%			
Q6 – Handling disruptive students	African American		(1)14.3%		(1)14.3%	(4)57.1%
	White					(1)14.3%
Q7 – Difference between major/minor infractions	African American	(1)12.5%	(2) 25%	(1)12.5%		(1)12.5%
	White					(1)12.5%
Q9 – Plan a basic lesson	African American	(1)12.5%		(1)12.5%	(3)37.5%	(2)25%
	White	(1)12.5%				
Q10 – Delivery of instruction	African American	(1)16.7%		(1)16.7%		(3)50%
	White			(1)16.7%		
Q16 – More than one training session per…	African American		(1)14.3%	(1)14.3%	(2)28.6%	
	White					(1)14.3%
Q18- Giving input on in-services	African American		(1)12.5%	(3)37.5%	(1)12.5%	(2) 25%
	White					(1)12.5%

74

Overall, there were several training questions that are important to African American's as well as White certified substitute teachers. The responses identified what certified substitute teachers say would be important in training for their effectiveness in the classroom. Knowing how to create a management plan, handling disruptive students, knowing how to plan a basic lesson, and having input in in-services are among the top percentiles of importance.

Table 3.2 shows the response from the certified substitute teacher based on grades taught and percentages of importance for each question.

Grades Taught

Q5 – When asked about training on writing a classroom management plan 1 or 12.5% of certified substitute teachers teaching grades 3-5 said this is important. 2 or 25% of certified substitute teachers teaching all grades (K-8) said this is least important and somewhat important. 3 or 37.5% said this is important.

Q6 – When asked about training on how to handle disruptive students 1 or 14.3% of certified substituted teachers teaching all grades said this is least important and important. 5 or 71.4% said this is especially important. All respondents did not answer this question.

Q7 – When asked about training on how to determine the difference between major and minor infractions 1 or 12.5% of certified substitute teachers teaching grades 3-5 said this is not important. 1 or 12.5% of certified substitute teachers teaching all grades said this is not important, least important, and somewhat important. 2 or 25% said this is important and especially important.

Q9 – When asked about having training on how to plan a basic lesson 1 or 12.5% of certified substitute teachers teaching grades 3-5 said this is especially important. 2 or 25% of certified substitute teachers teaching all grades said this is not important. 1 or 12.5% said this is somewhat important and especially important. 3 or 37.5% said this is important.

Q10 – When asked about training on how to deliver instruction 1 or 16.7% of certified substitute teachers teaching all grades said this is not important. 2 or 33.3% said this is somewhat important, while 3 or 50% said this is important. All respondents did answer this question.

Q16 – When asked about having training more than once a year 1 or 14.3% of certified substitute teachers teaching all grade said this is least important and somewhat important. 2 or 28.6% said this is important and 3 or 42.9% said this is especially important. All respondents did not answer this question.

Q18 – When asked about giving input on training for in-services 1 or 12.5% of certified substitute teachers teaching grades 3-5 said this is least important. 3 or 37.5% of certified substitute teachers teaching all grades said this is somewhat important and especially important, and 1 or 12.5% said this is important.

Table 3.2 – (TR)/Grades Taught - Importance

Question	Graded Taught	Not important	Least important	Somewhat important	Important	Especially important
Q5 – Classroom management plan	Grades 3-5				(1)12.5%	
	All (K-8)		(2) 25%	(2) 25%	(3)37.5%	
Q6 – Handling disruptive students	Grades 3-5					
	All (K-8)		(1)14.3%		(5)71.4%	
Q7 – Difference between major/minor infractions	Grades 3-5	(1)12.5%				
	All (K-8)	(1)12.5%	(1)12.5%	(1)12.5%	(2) 25%	(2) 25%
Q9 – Plan a basic lesson	Grades 3-5					(1)12.5%
	All (K-8)	(2)25%		(1)12.5%	(3)37.5%	(1)12.5%
Q10 – Delivery of instruction	Grades 3-5					
	All (K-8)	(1)16.7%		(2)33.3%	(3)50%	
Q16 – More than one training session per…	Grades 3-5					
	All (K-8)		(1)14.3%	(1)14.3%	(2)28.6%	(3)42.9%
Q18- Giving input on in-services	Grades 3-5		(1)12.5%			
	All (K-8)			(3)37.5%	(1)12.5%	(3)37.5%

Overall, there were several training issues that are of important to the certified

substitute teachers who taught grades K-8. The responses identified what certified substitute teachers say would be important in training for their effectiveness in the classroom. Handling disruptive students, differentiating between major and minor infractions, creating a basic lesson, delivering instruction, having more training sessions, and giving input in in-service topics top the list of importance.

Table 3.3 shows the response from the certified substitute teacher based on years of experience and the percentages of importance for each question.

Years of Substituting

Q5 – When asked about training on writing a classroom management plan 2 or 25% of certified substitutes teaching for 1-3 years said this is not important and 1 or 12.5% said this is important, 1 or 12.5% of certified substitute teachers teaching 3-5 years said this is somewhat important. 1 or 12.5% of certified substitute teachers teaching 7-10 years said this is somewhat important and important. 2 or 25% of certified substitute teachers teaching for more than 10 years said this is important.

Q6 – When asked about training on how to handle disruptive students 1 or 14.3% of certified substitutes teaching 1-3 years said this is least important and 2 or 28.6% said this is especially important. 1 or 14.3% of certified substitute teachers teaching 3-5 years said this is especially important. 1 or 14.3% of certified substitute teachers teaching 7-10 years this is especially important. 1 or 14.3% teaching 10 or more years said this is important and especially important. All respondents did not answer this question. All respondents did not answer this question.

Q7 –When asked about training on how to determine the difference between major and minor infractions 1 or 12.5% of certified substitute teachers teaching 1-3 years said this is not important and especially important. 1 or 12.5% of certified substitute teachers teaching 3-5 years said this is somewhat important. 1 or 12.5% of certified substitute teachers teaching 7-10 years said this is least important and important. 1 or 12.5% of certified substitute teachers teaching 10 or more years said this is important and 1 or 12.5% said this is especially important.

Q9 – When asked about having training on how to plan a basic lesson 2 or 25% of certified substitute teachers teaching 1-3 years said this is not important and 1 or 12.5% said this is especially important. 1 or 12.5% of certified substitute teachers teaching 3-5 years said this is especially important. 1 or 12.5% of certified substitute teachers teaching 7-10 years said this is important and particularly important. 1 or 12.5% of certified substitute teachers teaching 10 or more years said this is somewhat important and important.

Q10 – When asked about training on how to deliver instruction 1 or 16.7% of certified substitute teachers teaching 1-3 years said this is not important, somewhat important and important. 1 or 16.76% of certified substitute teachers teaching 3-5 years said this is important. 1 or 16.7% of certified substitute teachers teaching 7-10 years said this is important. 1 or 16.7% of certified substitute teachers teaching 10 or more years said this is somewhat important. All respondents did not answer this question.

Q16 – When asked about having training more than once a year 1 or 14.3% of certified substitutes teaching 1-3 years said this is least important and 2 or 28.6% said this is especially important. 1 or 14.3% of certified substitute teachers teaching 3-5 years said this especially important. 1 or 14.3% of certified substitute teachers teaching 7-10 years said this is somewhat important. 2 or 28.6% of certified substitute teachers teaching 10 or more years said this is important. All respondents did not answer this question.

Q18 – When asked about giving input on training for in-services 1 or 12.5% of certified substitutes teaching 1-3 years said this is somewhat important. 2 or 25% of certified substitute teachers teaching 3-5 years said this is important. 1 or 12.5% of certified substitute teachers teaching 7-10 ears said this is least important and somewhat important. 1 or 12.5% of certified substitute teachers teaching 10 or more years said this is somewhat important and especially important.

Table 3.3 – (TR)/Years of Substituting - Importance

Question	Years of Substituting	Not important	Least important	Somewhat important	Important	Especially important
Q5 – Classroom management plan	1-3 years	(2)25%			(1)12.5%	
	3-5 years			(1)12.5%		
	7-10 years			(1)12.5%	(1)12.5%	
	10 or more years				(2) 25%	
Q6 – Handling disruptive students	1-3 years		(1)14.3%			(2)28.6%
	3-5 years					(1)14.3%
	7-10 years					(1)14.3%
	10 or more years				(1)14.3%	(1)14.3%
Q7 – Difference between major/minor infractions	1-3 years	(1)12.5%				(1)12.5%
	3-5 years			(1)12.5%		
	7-10 years	(1)12.5%				
	10 or more years				(1)12.5%	
Q9 – Plan a basic lesson	1-3 years	(2)25%				(1)12.5%
	3-5 years				(1)12.5%	
	7-10 years				(1)12.5%	(1)12.5%
	10 or more years			(1)12.5%	(1)12.5%	
Q10 – Delivery of instruction	1-3 years	(1)16.7%		(1)16.7%	(1)16.7%	
	3-5 years					
	7-10 years				(1)16.7%	
	10 or more years			(1)16.7%		
Q16 – More than one training session per…	1-3 years	(1)14.3%				(2)28.6%
	3-5 years					(1)14.3%
	7-10 years			(1)14.3%		
	10 or more years				(2)28.6%	
Q18- Giving input on in-services	1-3 years			(1)12.5%		(2) 25%
	3-5 years				(1)12.5%	
	7-10 years		(1)12.5%			
	10 or more years			(1)12.5%		(1)12.5%

Overall, there were several training issues that are important to certified substitute teachers regardless of years of experience. The responses identified what certified substitute teachers say would be important in training for their effectiveness in the classroom. Having a classroom management plan, handling disruptive students, being able to create a basic lesson plan, more training, and input in in-services top the list of importance.

Table 3.4 shows the response from the certified substitute teacher based on the type of substitute position and the percentages of importance for each question.

Type of Substituting

Q5 – When asked about training on writing a classroom management plan 1 or 12.5% of day to day certified substitute teachers said this is least important and important. 1 or 12.5% of certified substitute teachers teaching in all positions said this is somewhat important and 3 or 37.5% said this is important. 1 or 12.5% of day to day and floater substitute teachers said this is least important. 1 or 12.5% of day to day and permanent substitute teachers said this is somewhat important.

Q6 – When asked about training on how to handle disruptive students 1 or 14.3% of day to day certified substitute teachers said this is least important, important and especially important. 1 or 14.3% of certified substitute teachers teaching in all positions said this is important and 2 or 28.6% said this is especially important. 1 or 14.3% of day to day and floater substitute teachers said this is especially important. 1 or 14.3% of day to day and permanent substitute teachers said this is especially important. All respondents did not answer this question.

Q7 – When asked about having training on how to determine the difference between a major and minor infraction 1 or 12.5% of day to day certified substitute teachers said this is not important and least important. 1 or 12.5% of certified substitute teachers teaching in all positions said this is least important, somewhat important, important and especially important. 1 or 12.5% of day to day and floater substitute teachers said this is especially important. 1 or 12.5% of day to day and permanent substitute teachers said this is important.

Q9 – When asked about having training on how to plan a basic lesson 1 or 12.5% of day to day certified substitute teachers said this is not important and especially important. 1 or 12.5% of certified substitute teachers teaching all positions said this is somewhat important and especially important. 1 or 12.5% said this is somewhat important and especially important.2 or 25% said this is important. 1 or 12.5% of day to day and floater substitute teachers said this is not important. 1 or 12.5% of day to day and permanent substitute teachers said this is important.

Q10 – When asked about training on how to deliver instruction 1 or 16.7% of day to day certified substitute teachers said this is not important and important. 1 or 16.7% of certified substitute teachers teaching all positions said this is somewhat important and especially important. 1 or 16.7% of day to day and floater substitute teachers said this is somewhat important. 1 or 16.7% of day to day and permanent substitute teachers said this is important. All respondents did not answer this question.

83

Q16 – When asked about having training more than one a year 1 or 14.3% of day to day certified substitute teachers said this is least important and especially important. 2 or 28.6% of certified substitute teachers teaching in all positions said this is important, 1 or 14.3% said this is especially important. 1 or 14.3% of day to day and floater substitute teachers said this is especially important. 1 or 14.3% of day to day and permanent substitute teachers said this is somewhat important. All respondents did not answer this question.

Q18- When asked about giving input on training for in-service 1 or 12.5% of day to day substitute teachers said this is somewhat important and especially important. 1 or 12.5% teaching all positions said this is least important, somewhat important, important and especially important. 1 or 12.5% of day to day and floater substitutes said this is especially important. 1 or 12.5 % of day to day and permanent substitute teachers said this is somewhat important.

Table 3.4 – (TR)/Type of Substituting - Importance

Question	Type of substituting	Not important	Least important	Somewhat important	Important	Especially important
Q5 –Classroom management plan	Day to day		(1)12.5%		(1)12.5%	
	All			(1)12.5%	(3)37.5%	
	Day to day/floater		(1)12.5%			
	Day to day/permanent			(1)12.5%		
Q6 – Handling disruptive students	Day to day		(1)14.3%			(1)14.3%
	All				(1)14.3%	(2)28.6%
	Day to day/floater					(1)14.3%
	Day to day/permanent					(1)14.3%
Q7 – Difference between major/minor infractions	Day to day	(1)12.5%	(1)12.5%			(1)12.5%
	All		(1)12.5%	(1)12.5%	(1)12.5%	(1)12.5%
	Day to day/floater					
	Day to day/permanent				(1)12.5%	
Q9 – Plan a basic lesson	Day to day	(1)12.5%				(1)12.5%
	All			(1)12.5%	(2)25%	(1)12.5%
	Day to day/floater	(1)12.5%				
	Day to day/permanent					(1)12.5%
Q10 – Delivery of instruction	Day to day	(1)16.7%			(1)16.7%	
	All			(1)16.7%		(1)16.7%
	Day to day/floater			(1)16.7%		
	Day to day/permanent					(1)16.7%
Q16 – More than one training session per…	Day to day		(1)14.3%			(1)14.3%
	All				(2)28.6%	(1)14.3%
	Day to day/floater					(1)14.3%
	Day to day/permanent				(1)14.3%	
Q18- Giving input on in-services	Day to day			(1)12.5%		(1)12.5%
	All		(1)12.5%5	(1)12.5%	(1)12.5%	(1)12.5%
	Day to day/floater					(1)12.5%
	Day to day/permanent			(1)12.5%		

Overall, there were several training issues that are important to certified substitute teachers teaching in all positions. The responses identified what certified substitute teachers would be important in training for their effectiveness in the classroom. Having a classroom management plan, handling disruptive students, creating a basic lesson, delivery of instruction, and more training sessions top the list of importance.

Table 3.5 shows the response from the certified substitute teacher based on certified substitute teachers that have gone through the district training program and the percentages of importance for each question.

Trained Substitutes

Q5 – When asked about training on writing a classroom management plan 2 or 25% said this is least important and somewhat important. 4 or 50% said this is important.

Q6 – When asked about training on how to handle disruptive students 1 or 14.3% said this is least important and important, while 5 or 71.4% said this is especially important. All respondents did not answer this question.

Q7 – When asked about training on how to determine the difference between major and minor infractions 1 or 12.5% said this is not important, somewhat important, important, and especially important. While 2 or 25% said this is important and especially important

Q9 – When asked about having training on how to plan a basic lesson 2 or 25% said this is not important and especially important. 1 or 12.5% said this is somewhat important and 3 or 37.5% said this is important.

Q10 – When asked about training on how to deliver instructions 1 or 16.7% said this is not important. 2 or 33.3% said this is somewhat important, while 3 or 50% said this is important. All respondents did not answer this question.

Q16 – When asked about having training more than one a year 1 or 14.3% said this is least important and somewhat important. 2 or 28.6% said this is important and 3 or 42.9% said this is especially important. All respondents did not answer this question.

Q18 – When asked about giving input on training for in-services 1 or 12.5% said this is least important and important, while 3 or 37.5% said this is somewhat important and especially important.

Table 3.5– (TR)/Trained Substitutes - Importance

Question	Trained Substitutes	Not important	Least important	Somewhat important	Important	Especially important
Q5 –Classroom management plan			(2) 25%	(2)25%	(4)50%	
Q6 – Handling disruptive students			(1)14.3%		(1)14.3%	(5)71.4%
Q7 – Difference between major/minor infractions		(1)12.5%	(2) 25%	(1)12.5%	(2) 25%	(2) 25%
Q9 – Plan a basic lesson		(2) 25%		(1)12.5%	(3)37.5%	(2) 25%
Q10 – Delivery of instruction		(1)16.7%		(2)33.3%	(3)50%	
Q16 – More than one training session per…			(1)14.3%	(1)14.3%	(2)28.6%	(3)42.9%
Q18- Giving input on in-services			(1)12.5%	(3)37.5%	(1)12.5%	(3)37.5%

87

Overall, there are several training issues that are important to certified substitute teachers. Who have gone through the districts training program? The responses identified what certified substitute teachers say would be important in training for their effectiveness in the classroom. Handling disruptive students, creating a basic lesson, delivering instruction, and more training sessions, top the list of importance.

Classroom Management

Four questions from the survey were coded under the category of classroom management Q8, Q11, Q12, and Q13. Using SPSS statistical software package, the researcher examined and compared the importance of each question based on the rating give by the respondent. Rank scores used for the survey were:

1=not important 2=least important 3=somewhat important 4= important 5= especially important.

Table 4 shows the response from the certified substitute teacher based on gender and the percentages of importance for each question.

Gender

Q8 – When asked about making phone calls home 1 or 16.7% of males said this is not important. 2 or 33.3% of males said this is especially important. 1 or 16.7% of females said this is somewhat important, important, and especially important. All respondents did not answer this question.

Q11 – When asked about keeping students attentive and engaged 1 or 12.5% of males said this is least important and 2 or 25% said this is important. 3 or 37.5% of females said this is important and 2 or 25% said this is especially important.

Q12 – When asked about transitioning from one class to another 1 or 12.5% of males said this is not important, least important and important. 1 or 12.5% of females said this is least important and 2 or 25% said this is somewhat important and important.

Q13 – When asked about transitioning from one subject to another 1 or 12.5 % of males said this is not important, somewhat important and important. 1 or 12.5% of females said this is least important and somewhat important, while 3 or 37.5% said this is important.

Table 4 – (CM)/Gender - Importance

Question	Gender	Not important	Least important	Somewhat important	Important	Especially important
Q8 – Making phone calls home.	Male	(1)16.7%				(2)33.3%
	Female			(1)16.7%	(1)16.7%	(1)16.7%
Q11 – Engaging students in lessons	Male		(1)12.5%		(2) 25% (3)37.5%	(2) 25%
	Female					
Q12 – Transition from class to class	Male	(1)12.5%	(1)12.5%		(1)12.5% (2) 25%	
	Female	(1)12.5%		(2) 25%		
Q13 – Transition from subject to subject	Male	(1)12.5%		(1)12.5%	(1)12.5%	
	Female	(1)12.5%		(1)12.5%		(3)37.5%

Overall, there were several classroom managements issues that are important to both male and female certified substitute teachers. The responses identified what certified substitute teachers say would be important in training for their effectiveness in the classroom. Knowing when to make phone calls home, having engaging lessons for students and being able to transition from subject to subject top the list of importance.

Table 4.1 shows the response from the certified substitute teacher based on both races and percentages of importance for each question.

Race

Q8 – When asked about making phone calls home 1 or 16.7% of African Americans said this is not important, somewhat important, and important. 2 or 33.3% said this is especially important. 1 or 16.7% of Whites said this is especially important. All respondents did not answer this question.

Q11 – When asked about keeping students attentive and engaged 1 or 12.5% of African Americans said this is least important and especially important, while 5 or 62.5% said this is important. 1 or 12.5% of Whites said this is especially important.

Q12 – When asked about transitioning from one class to another 1 or 12.5% of African Americans said this is not important and least important. 2 or 25% said this is somewhat important and 3 or 37.5% said this is important. 1 or 12.5% of Whites said this is least important.

Q13 – When asked about transitioning from one subject to another 1 or 12.5% of African Americans said this is not important. 2 or 25% said this is somewhat important and 4 or 50% said this is important. 1 or 12.5% of Whites said this is least important.

Table 4.1 – (CM)/Race- Importance

Question	Race	Not important	Least important	Somewhat important	Important	Especially important
Q8 – Making phone calls home.	African American	(1)16.7%		(1)16.7%	(1)16.7%	(2)33.3%
	White					(1)16.7%
Q11 – Engaging students in lessons	African American		(1)12.5%			(1)12.5%
	White				(5)62.5%	(1)12.5%5
Q12 – Transition from class to class	African American	(1)12.5%	(1)12.5%	(2) 25%	(3)37.5%	
	White		(1)12.5%			
Q13 – Transition from subject to subject	African American	(1)12.5%		(2) 25%	(4)50%	
	White		(1)12.5%			

Overall, there are several classroom managements issues that are important to African American's and White certified substitute teachers. The responses identified what certified substitute teachers say would be important in training for their effectiveness in the classroom. Making calls home, engaging students, and transitioning from class to class and subject to subject topped the list.

Table 4.2 shows the response from the certified substitute teacher based on grades taught and percentages of importance for each question.

Grades Taught

Q8 – When asked about making phone calls home 1 or 16.7% of certified substitutes teaching all grades (K-8) said this is not important, least important, and important, and 3 or 50% said this is important. All respondents did not answer this question.

Q11 – when asked about keeping students attentive and engaged 1 or 12.5% of certified substitutes teaching grades 3-5 said this is especially important. 1 or 12.5% of certified substitute teachers teaching all positions said this is least important and especially important 5 or 62.5% said this is important.

Q12 – When asked about transitioning from one class to another 1 or 12.5% of certified substitute teachers teaching grades 3-5 said this is somewhat important. 1 or 12.5% of certified substitute teachers teaching all positions said this is not important and somewhat important. 2 or 25% said this is least important and 3 or 37.5% said this is important.

Q13 – When asked about transitioning from one subject to another 1 or 12.5% of certified substitutes teaching grades 3-5 said this is important. 1 or 12.5% of certified substitute teachers teaching all grades said this is not important and least important. 2 or 25% said this is somewhat important and 3 or 37.5% said this is important.

Table 4.2 – (TR)/Grades Taught - Importance

Questions	Graded Taught	Not important	Least important	Somewhat important	Important	Especially important
Q8 – Making phone calls home.	Grades 3-5					
	All (K-8)	(1)16.7%	(1)16.7%		(1)16.7%	(3) 50%
Q11 – Engaging students in lessons	Grades 3-5					(1)12.5%
	All (K-8)		(1)12.5%		(5)62.5%	(1)12.5%
Q12 – Transition from class to class	Grades 3-5			(1)12.5%		
	All (K-8)	(1)12.5%	(2)25%	(1)12.5%	(3)37.5%	
Q13 – Transition from subject to subject	Grades 3-5				(1)12.5%	
	All (K-8)	(1)12.5%	(1)12.5%	(2) 25%	(3)37.5%	

Overall, there were several classroom managements issues that are important to certified substitute teachers that taught all grades. The responses identified what certified substitute teachers say would be important in training for their effectiveness in the classroom. Again, making phone calls home, engaging students, making transitions from class to class and subject to subject are important to the participants of this study.

Table 4.3 shows the response from the certified substitute teacher based on teaching experience and the percentages of importance for each question.

93

Years Substituting

Q8 – When asked about making phone calls home 1 or 16.7% of certified substitute teachers who taught 1-3 years said this is not important and 2 or 33.3% said this is especially important. 1 or 16.7% of certified substitute teachers teaching 3-5 years said this is somewhat important. 1 or 16.7% of certified substitute teachers teaching 7-10 years said this is especially important. 1 or 16.7% of certified substitute teachers teaching 10 or more years said this is important. All respondents did not answer this question.

Q11 – When asked about keeping students attentive and engaged 1 or 12.5% of certified substitute teachers who taught 1-3 years said this is least important, important, and especially important. 1 or 12.5% of certified substitute teachers teaching 3-5 years said this is important. 1 or 12.5% of certified substitute teachers teaching 7-10 years said this is important and especially important. 2 or 25% of certified substitute teachers teaching 10 or more years said this is important.

Q12 – When asked about transitioning from one class to another 1 or 12.5% of certified substitute teachers who taught 1-3 years said this is not important and 2 or 25% said this is least important. 1 or 12.5% of certified substitute teachers teaching 3-5 years said this is somewhat important. 1 or 12.5% of certified substitute teachers teaching 7-10 years said this is somewhat important and important. 2 or 25% of certified substitute teachers teaching 10 or more years said this is important.

Q13 – When asked about transitioning from one subject to another 1 or 12.5% of certified substitute teachers who taught 1-3 years said this is not important, least important, and important. 1 or 12.5% of certified substitute teachers teaching 3-5 years said this is important. 1 or 12.5% of certified substitute teachers teaching 7-10 years said this is somewhat important and important. 1 or 12.5% of certified substitute teachers teaching 10 or more years said this is somewhat important and important.

Table 4.3 – (TR)/Years of Substituting - Importance

Question	Years of Substituting	Not important	Least important	Somewhat important	Important	Especially important
Q8 – Making phone calls home.	1-3 years	(1)16.7%				(2)33.3%
	3-5 years			(1)16.7%		
	7-10 years					(1)12.5%
	10 or more years				(2) 25%	
Q11 – Engaging students in lessons	1-3 years	(1)12.5%			(1)12.5%	(1)12.5%
	3-5 years				(1)12.5%	
	7-10 years				(1)12.5%	(1)12.5%
	10 or more years				(2) 25%	
Q12 – Transition from class to class	1-3 years	(1)12.5%	(2)25%			
	3-5 years			(1)12.5%		
	7-10 years			(1)12.5%	(1)12.5%	
	10 or more years				(2) 25%	
Q13 – Transition from subject to subject	1-3 years	(1)12.5%	(1)12.5%		(1)12.5%	
	3-5 years				(1)12.5%	
	7-10 years			(1)12.5%	(1)12.5%	
	10 or more years			(1)12.5%	(1)12.5%	

Overall, there were several classroom managements issues that are important to certified substitute teachers regardless of the number of years worked. The responses identified what certified substitute teachers say would be important in training for their effectiveness in the classroom. Knowing when to make phone calls home, engaging students, and transitioning from class to class and subject to subject is important to certified substitute teachers regardless of how long they had taught.

Table 4.4 shows the response from the certified substitute teacher based on the type of position and the percentages of importance for each question.

Type of Substituting

Q8 –When asked about making phone calls home 1 or 16.7% of day to day certified substitute teachers said this is not important and especially important. 1 or 16.7% of certified substitute teachers teaching all positions (K-8) said this is somewhat important and important. 1 or 16.7% of day to day and floater substitute teachers said this is especially important. 1 or 16.7% of day to day and permanent substitute teachers said this is especially important. All respondents did not answer this question.

Q11 – When asked about keeping students attentive and engaged 1 or 12.5% of day to day certified substitute teachers said this is least important and important. 3 or 37.5% of certified substitute teachers teaching all positions said this is important and 1 or 12.5% said this is especially important. 1 or 12.5% of day to day and floater substitute teachers said this is especially important. 1 or 12.5% of day to day and permanent substitute teachers said this is important.

Q12 – When asked about transitioning from one class to another 1 or 12.5% of day to day certified substitute teachers said this is not important and least important. 2 or 25% of certified substitute teachers teaching all positions said this is somewhat important and important. 1 or 12.5% of day to day and floater substitute teachers said this is least important. 1 or 12.5% of day to day and permanent substitute teachers said this is important.

Q13 – When asked about transitioning from subject to subject 1 or 12.5% of day to day certified substitutes said this is not important and important. 1 or 12.5% of certified substitute teachers teaching all positions said this is somewhat important and 3 or 37.5% said this is important. 1 or 12.5% of day to day and floater substitute teachers said this is least important. 1 or 12.5% of day to day and permanent substitute teachers said this is somewhat important.

Table 4.4 – (TR)/Types of Substituting - Importance

Question	Types of Substituting	Not important	Least important	Somewhat important	Important	Especially important
Q8 – Making phone calls home.	Day to day All Day to day/floater Day to day/permanent	(1)16.7%		(1)16.7%	(1)16.7%	(1)16.7% (1)16.7% (1)16.7%
Q11 – Engaging students in lessons	Day to day All Day to day/floater Day to day/permanent		(1)12.5%		(1)12.5% (3)37.5% (1)12.5%	(1)12.5% (1)12.5%
Q12 – Transition from class to class	Day to day All Day to day/floater Day to day/permanent	(1)12.5%	(1)12.5% (1)12.5%	(2) 25%	(2) 25% (2) 25%	
Q13 – Transition from subject to subject	Day to day All Day to day/floater Day to day/permanent	(1)12.5%	 (1)12.5%	(1)12.5% (1)12.5%	(1)12.5% (3)37.5%	

Overall, there were several classroom managements issues that are important to certified substitute teachers who taught in all areas. The responses identified what certified substitute teachers say would be important in training for their effectiveness in the classroom. Making phone calls home, engaging students, transitioning from class to class and subject to subject have the highest percentages as to its importance to certified substitute teacher.

Table 4.5 shows the response from the certified substitute teacher who have gone through the training program and the percentages of importance for each question.

Trained Substitutes

Q8 – When asked about making phone calls home 1 or 16.7% said this is not important, somewhat important, and important and 3 or 50% said this is especially important. All respondents did not answer this question.

Q11 – When asked about keeping student attentive and engaged 1 or 12.5% said this is least important. 5 or 62.5% said this is important and 2 or 25% said this is especially important.

Q12 – When asked about transitioning from one class to another 1 or 12.5% said this is not important. 2 or 25% said this is least important and 3 or 37.5% said this is important.

Q13 – When asked about transitioning from one subject to another 1 or 12.5% said this is not important and least important. 2 or 25% said this is somewhat important, while 4 or

50% said this is important.

Table 4.5 – (TR)/Trained Substitutes - Importance

Question	Trained Substitutes	Not important	Least important	Somewhat important	Important	Especially important
Q8 – Making phone calls home.		(1)16.7%		(1)16.7%	(1)16.7%	(3)50%
Q11 – Engaging students in lessons			(1)12.5%		62.5%	25%
Q12 – Transition from class to class		(1)12.5%	(2) 25%	(2)25%	(3)37.5%	
Q13 – Transition from subject to subject		(1)12.5%	(1)12.5%	(2)25%	(4) 50%	

Overall, there were several training issues that are important to certified substitute teachers who had gone through the district training program. The responses identified what certified substitute teachers say would be important in training for their effectiveness in the classroom. Making calls home, engaging students, and being able to transition from class to class and subject to subject are all of importance.

Classroom Procedures

Four questions from the survey were coded under the category of classroom procedures.

99

Q20, Q21, Q22, and Q23. Using SPSS statistical software package, the researcher

examined and compared the importance of each question based on the rating give by the

respondent. Rank scores used for the survey were:

1=not important 2=least important 3=somewhat important 4= important   5= especially

important.

Table 5 shows the response from the certified substitute teacher based on both

genders and the percentages of importance for each question.

Gender

Q20 – When asked about classroom procedures 1 or 12.5% of males said this is

important. 2 or 25% said this is especially important. 25% of females said this is

important. 3 or 37.5% said this is especially important.

Q21 – When asked about knowing staff members to contact 1 or 12.5% of males said this

is somewhat important, important, and especially important. 2 or 25% of females said this

is important and 3 or 37.5% said this is especially important.

Q22- When asked about contacting the office in case of emergencies 1 or 12.5% of males

said this is somewhat important and 2 or 25% said this is especially important. 1 or

12.5% of females said this is important and 4 or 50% said this is especially important.

Q23 – When asked about knowing the emergency drill procedures 3 or 37.5% of males

said this is especially important. 1 or 12.5% of females said this is important while 4 or

50% said this is especially important.

Table 5 – (CP)/Gender - Importance

Question	Gender	Not important	Least important	Somewhat important	Important	Especially important
Q20 – Appropriate classroom procedures.	Male				1(1)2.5%	(2)25%
	Female				(2) 25%	(3)37.5%
Q21 – Staff members to ask questions.	Male			(1)12.5%	(1)12.5%	(1)12.5%
	Female				(2) 25%	(3)37.5%
Q22 – Office contact for emergencies,	Male			(1)12.5%		(2) 25%
	Female				(1)12.5%	(4) 50%
Q23 – Emergency drill procedures.	Male					(3)37.5%
	Female				(1)12.5%	(4) 50%

Overall, there were several classroom procedures that are important to both male and female certified substitute teachers. The responses identified what certified substitute teachers say would be important in training for their effectiveness in the classroom. Knowing appropriate classroom procedures, knowing staff members, knowing office contacts and emergency drill procedures are of great importance to the certified substitute teacher.

Table 5.1 shows the response from the certified substitute teacher based on both races and the percentages of importance for each question.

Race

Q20 – When asked about classroom procedures 3 or 37.5% of African Americans said this is important and 4 or 50% said this is especially important. 1 or 12.5% of Whites said this is especially important.

Q21 – When asked about knowing staff members to contact 1 or 12.5% of African Americans said this is somewhat important while 3 or 37.5% said this is important and especially important. 1 or 12.5% of Whites said this is especially important.

Q22 – When asked about contacting the office in case of emergencies 1 or 12.5% of African Americans said this is somewhat important and important while 5 or 62.5% said this is especially important. 1 or 12.5% of Whites said this is especially important.

Q23 – When asked about knowing the emergency drill procedures 1 or 12.5% of African Americans said this is important and 6 or 75% said this is especially important. 1 or 12.5% of Whites said this is especially important.

Table 5.1 – (CP)/Race - Importance

Question	Race	Not important	Least important	Somewhat important	Important	Especially important
Q20 – Appropriate classroom procedures.	African American				(3)37.5%	(4) 50%
	White					(1)12.5%
Q21 – Staff members to ask questions.	African American			(1)12.5%	(3)37.5%	(3)37.5%
	White					(1)12.5%
Q22 – Office contact for emergencies,	African American			(1)12.5%	(1)12.5%	(5)62.5%
	White					(1)12.5%
Q23 – Emergency drill procedures.	African American				(1)12.5%	(6) 75%
	White					(1)12.5%

Overall, there were several classroom procedures that are important to African American's as well as for White certified substitute teachers. The responses identified what certified substitute teachers say would be important in training for their effectiveness in the classroom. Again, all four questions were of importance to the participants.

Table 5.2 shows the response from the certified substitute teacher based on grades taught and the percentages of importance for each question.

Grades Taught

Q20 – When asked about classroom procedures 1 or 12.5% of certified substitutes teaching grades 3-5 said this is especially important. 3 or 37.5% of certified substitute teachers teaching all grades (K-8) said this is important and 4 or 50% said this is especially important.

Q21 – When asked about knowing staff members to contact 1 or 12.5% of certified substitutes teaching grades 3-5 said this is especially important. 1 or 12.5% of certified substitute teachers teaching all grades said this is somewhat important and 3 or 37.5% said this is important and especially important.

Q22 – When asked about contacting the office in case of emergencies 1 or 12.5% of certified substitutes teaching grades 3-5 said this is especially important. 1 or 12.5% of certified substitute teachers teaching all grades said this is somewhat important and important, while 5 or 62.5% said this is especially important.

103

Q23 – When asked about knowing the emergency drill procedures 1 or 12.5% of certified substitutes teaching grades 3-5 said this is especially important. 1 or 12.5% of certified substitute teachers teaching all grades said this is important while 6 or 75% said this is especially important.

Table 5.2 – (CP)/Grades Taught - Importance

Question	Grades Taught	Not important	Least important	Somewhat important	Important	Especially important
Q20 – Appropriate classroom procedures.	Grades 3-5					(1)12.5%
	All (K-8)				(3)37.5%	(4) 50%
Q21 – Staff members to ask questions.	Grades 3-5					(1)12.5%
	All (K-8)			(1)12.5%	(3)37.5%	(3)37.5%
Q22 – Office contact for emergencies,	Grades 3-5					(1)12.5%
	All (K-8)			(1)12.5%	(1)12.5%5	(5)62.5%
Q23 – Emergency drill procedures.	Grades 3-5					(1)12.5%
	All (K-8)				(1)12.5%	(6) 75%

Overall, there were several classroom procedures that are important to certified substitute teachers who taught grades K-8. The responses identified what certified substitute teachers say would be important in training for their effectiveness in the classroom. At every grade level the substitute teachers found that knowing

classroom

procedures, having a staff member to ask questions of, how to contact the office, and knowing emergency procedures are important.

Table 5.3 shows the response from the certified substitute teacher based on years of experience and the percentages of importance for each question.

Years of Substituting

Q20 – When asked about classroom procedures 1 or 12.5% of certified substitute teachers teaching 1-3 years said this is important and 2 or 25% said this is especially important. 1 or 12.5% of certified substitute teachers teaching 3-5 years said this is important. 2 or 25% of certified substitute teachers teaching 7-10 years said this is especially important. 1 or 12.5% of certified substitute teachers teaching 10 or more years said this is important and especially important.

Q21 – When asked about knowing staff members to contact 1 or 12.5% of certified substitute teachers teaching 1-3 years said this is somewhat important, important and especially important. 1 or 12.5% of certified substitute teachers teaching 3-5 years said this is important. 2 or 25% of certified substitute teachers teaching 7-10 years said this is especially important. 1 or 12.5% of certified substitute teachers teaching 10 or more years said this is important and especially important.

Q22 – When asked about contacting the office in case of emergencies 1 or 12.5% of certified substitute teachers teaching 1-3 years said this is somewhat important and 2 or 25% said this is especially important. 1 or 12.5% of certified substitute teachers teaching 3-5 years said this is especially important. 2 or 25% of certified substitute teachers teaching 7-10 years said this is especially important. 1 or 12.5% of certified substitute teachers teaching 10 or more years said this is important and especially important.

Q23 – When asked about knowing the emergency drill procedures 3 or 37.5% of certified substitute teachers teaching 1-3 years said this is especially important. 1 or 12.5% of certified substitute teachers teaching 3-5 years said this is especially important. 2 or 25% of certified substitute teachers teaching 7-10 years said this is especially important. 1 or 12.5% of certified substitute teachers teaching 10 or more years said this is important and especially important.

Table 5.3 – (CP)/Years of Substituting - Importance

Question	Years of Experience	Not important	Least important	Somewhat important	Important	Especially important
Q20 – Appropriate classroom procedures.	1-3 years 3-5 years 7-10 years 10 or more years				(1)12.5% (1)12.5% (1)12.5%	(2) 25% (2) 25% (1)12.5%
Q21 – Staff members to ask questions.	1-3 years 3-5 years 7-10 years 10 or more years			(1)12.5%	(1)12.5% (1)12.5% (1)12.5%	 (2) 25% (1)12.5%
Q22 – Office contact for emergencies,	1-3 years 3-5 years 7-10 years 10 or more years			(1)12.5%	 (1)12.5%	(2) 25% (1)12.5% (2) 25% (1)12.5%
Q23 – Emergency drill procedures.	1-3 years 3-5 years 7-10 years 10 or more years				 (1)12.5%	(3)37.5% (1)12.5% (2) 25% (1)12.5%

Overall, there were several classroom procedures that are important to certified substitute teachers regardless of the number of years taught. The responses identified what certified substitute teachers say would be important in training for their effectiveness in the classroom. Understanding appropriate classroom procedures, having a staff member to ask questions, knowing when to contact the office for emergencies, and knowing emergency building procedures ranked extremely high on the scale of importance.

Table 5.4 shows the response from the certified substitute teacher based on the type of substituting position and the percentages of importance for each question.

Type of Substituting

Q20 – When asked about classroom procedures 1 or 12.5% of day to day certified substitutes said this is important and especially important. 2 or 25% of certified substitute teachers in all positions said this is important and especially important. 1 or 12.5% of day to day and floater substitute teachers said this is especially important, 1 or 12.5% of day to day and permanent substitute teachers said this is especially important.

Q21 – When asked about knowing staff members to contact 1 or 12.5% of day to day certified substitute teachers said this is somewhat important and important. 2 or 25% of certified substitute teachers in all positions said this is important and especially important. 1 or 12.5% of day to day and floater substitute teachers said this is especially important. 1 or 12.5% of day to day and permanent substitute teachers said this is

107

especially important.

Q22 – When asked about contacting the office in case of emergencies 1 or 12.5% of day to day certified substitute teachers said this is somewhat important and especially important. 1 or 12.5% of certified substitute teachers in all positions said this is important while 3 or 37.5% said this is especially important. 1 or 12.5% of day to day and floater substitute teachers said this is especially important. 1 or 12.5% of day to day and permanent substitute teachers said this is especially important.

Q23 – When asked about knowing the emergency drill procedures 2 or 25% of day to day certified substitute teachers said this is especially important. 1 or 12.5% of certified substitute teachers in all positions said this is important, while 3 or 37.5% said this is especially important. 1 or 12.5% of day to day and floater substitute teachers this is especially important. 1 or 12.5% of day to day and permanent substitute teachers said this is especially important.

Table 5.4 – (CP)/Type of Substituting - Importance

Question	Type of Position	Not important	Least important	Somewhat important	Important	Especially important
Q20 – Appropriate classroom procedures.	Day to day All Day to day/floater Day to day/permanent				(1)12.5% (2) 25%	(1)12.5% (2) 25% (1)12.5% (1)12.5%
Q21 – Staff members to ask questions.	Day to day All Day to day/floater Day to day/permanent			(1)12.5%	(1)12.5% (2)25%	(2) 25% (1)12.5% (1)12.5%
Q22 – Office contact for emergencies,	Day to day All Day to day/floater Day to day/permanent			(1)12.5%	(1)12.5%	(3)37.5% (1)12.5% (1)12.5%
Q23 – Emergency drill procedures.	Day to day All Day to day/floater Day to day/permanent				(1)12.5%	(2) 25% (3)37.5% (1)12.5% (1)12.5%

Overall, there were several classroom procedures that are important to certified substitute teachers that taught in various positions. The responses identified what certified substitute teachers say would be important in training for their effectiveness in the classroom. As with the other variables, the type of position held did not change the level of importance of what certified substitute teachers said was needed to be effective in the classroom.

Table 5.5 shows the response from the certified substitute teacher based on completion of the district training program and the percentages of importance for each question.

Trained Substitutes

Q20 – When asked about classroom procedures 3 or 37.5% said this is important, while 5 or 62.5% said this is especially important.

Q21 – When asked about knowing staff members to contact 1 or 12.5% said this is somewhat important, while 3 or 37.5% said this is important and 4 or 50% said this is especially important.

Q22 – When asked about contacting the office in case of emergencies 1 or 12.5% said this is somewhat important and important, while 6 or 75% said this is especially important.

Q23 – When asked about knowing the emergency drill procedures 1 or 12.5% said this is important while 7 or 87.5% said this is especially important.

Table 5.5 – (CP)/Trained Substitutes- Importance

Question	Trained Substitute	Not important	Least important	Somewhat important	Important	Especially important
Q20 – Appropriate classroom procedures.					(3)37.5%	(5)62.5%
Q21 – Staff members to ask questions.				(1)12.5%	(3)37.5%	(4) 50%
Q22 – Office contact for emergencies,				(1)12.5%	(1)12.5%	(6) 75%
Q23 – Emergency drill procedures.					(1)12.5%	(7)87.5%

Overall, there were several classroom procedures that are important to certified substitute teachers who had gone through the district training program. The responses identified what certified substitute teachers say would be important in training for their effectiveness in the classroom. With overwhelming numbers certified substitute teachers say, understanding appropriate classroom procedures, having a staff member to ask questions of, knowing office emergency procedures, and knowing the emergency drill procedures are important based on the percentages showed in the above table.

Open-Ended Question Responses

The results of the open-ended question from study were based on responses from

111

the certified substitute teachers from a South Suburban school outside of a large Metropolitan area. Eight (8) or 11% of the respondents who completed the survey only two (2) 25% 1 or 50% male and 1 or 50% female responded to the open-ended question at the end of the survey questionnaire. The one major point that stood out for both respondents pertained to building procedures.

One spoke of being disrespected by administration and other staff members in most of the buildings they substituted in. On the other hand, there was one building where the professionalism was extremely high from the principal down to the students. Upon arriving at the school, a student would escort the substitute teacher around and show them where the washrooms, teacher and student lounges and other things that may be of importance were. The principal would come in and introduce or re-introduce the substitute teacher to the class and reinforce the school expectation while the substitute was in the building. This made the substitute feel like an important part of the staff and they felt they had administrative support, unlike in other buildings.

The other respondent spoke of taking courses in preparation of real-life situations that would be encountered by a substitute. The substitute teacher felt this should be done by all substitute teachers to help with classroom effectiveness. Even though there were only two who responded to the open-ended question the researcher believes some more insight was placed on what certified substitute teachers say is needed to be effective in the classroom.

Summary

Determining what certified substitute teachers said they needed to be effective in the classroom was the purpose for this study. Most certified substitute teachers surveyed for this study felt there is more to be done in training to help certified substitute teachers be more effective in the classroom.

Four categories of training were identified from the data collected based on the questions asked in the survey questionnaire. Building Procedures (BP), Training (TR), Classroom Management (CM), and Classroom Procedures (CP). Along with the cross tabulation of the different areas of the demographics section of the questionnaire for certified substitute teachers made their voice heard as to what they say is needed in training to be effective in the classroom. The top questions in each category that were identified as being important and especially important were placed in a chart. Chart 1 represents the findings for building procedures based on the percentages for each variable identified by the certified substitute teachers. Chart 2 represents the findings for training based on the percentages for each variable identified by the certified substitute teachers.

Chart 3 represents the findings for classroom management based on the percentages for each variable identified by the certified substitute teachers. Chart 4 represents the findings for classroom procedures based on the percentages for each variable identified by the certified substitute teachers. Each question was broken down and cross tabulated with, gender, race, years of experience, type of substitute position, and the district training program.

The survey instrument proved to be especially useful in finding out what certified substitute teachers said was needed to be effective in the classroom. Based on the responses and the percentages given areas certified substitute teachers have given insight on what they say is need in training to be effective. Certified substitute teachers said it well, and now their voices are accounted for and the data collected will help fill the gap in the literature. This study was based on the perspective of the certified substitute teacher, and all other studies or surveys found were from the perspective of the school district, administrators, and Sub managers, not the certified substitute teachers. The results were interesting and Chapter Five will address recommendations for future studies and training programs for certified substitute teachers.

Chart 1 Building Procedures/ Top questions of importance

Question #	Gender	Race	Grades Taught	Year Experience	Type	Trained
8 – Making calls home	(4)66.7%	(4)66.7%	(4)66.7%	(4)66.7%	(4)66.7%	(4)66.7%
11 – Engaging students in lesson	(7)87.5%	(7)87.5%	(7)87.5%	(7)87.5%	(7)87.5%	(7)87.5%
12 – Transition from class to class	(3)37.5%	(3)37.5%	(3)37.5%	(3)37.5%	(3)37.5%	(3)37.5%
13 – Transition from subject to subject	(4)50%	(4)50%	(4)50%	(4)50%	(4)50%	(4)50%

Chart 2 Training/Top questions of importance

Question #	Gender	Race	Grades Taught	Years' Experience	Type	Trained
1 – Attending Building Meetings	(5)62.5%	(5)62.5%	(5)62.5%	(5)62.5%	(5)62.5%	(5)62.5%
2 – Attending district in-services	(6)75%	(6)75%	(6)75%	(6)75%	(6)75%	(6)75%
4 – Written and verbal feedback	(4)50%	(4)50%	(4)50%	(5) 62.5%	(4)50%	(4)50%
14 – Bell schedule	(7)87.5%	(7)87.5%	(7)87.5%	(7)87.5%	(7)87.5%	(7)87.5%
15 – Master bell schedule	(5)62.5%	(5)62.5%	(5)62.5%	(5)62.5%	(5)62.5%	(5)62.5%
17 – Feeling like a part of the staff	(7)87.5%	(7)87.5%	(7)87.5%	(7)87.5%	(7)87.5%	(7)87.5%
19 – Knowing appropriate building procedures	(8)100%	(8)100%	(8)100%	(7)87.5%	(8)100%	(8)100%

Chart 3 Classroom Management/Top questions of importance

Question #	Gender	Race	Grades Taught	Years Experience	Type	Trained
5 – Classroom Management Rules	(4)50%	(4)50%	(4)50%	(4)50%	(4)50%	(4)50%
6 – Handling disruptive behavior	(6)83.8%	(6)85.7%	(5)71.4%	(6)85.7%	(6)85.7%	(6)85.7%
7 – Difference between major and minor infractions	(4)50%	(4)50%	(4)50%	(4)50%	(4)50%	(4)50%
9 – Plan a basic lesson	(5)62.5%	(5)62.5%	(5)62.5%	(5)62.5%	(5)62.5%	(5)62.5%
10 – Delivery of instruction	(3)50%	(3)50%	(3)50%	(3)50%	(3)50%	(3)50%
16 – More than one training session	(5)71.5%	(5)71.5%	(5)71.5%	(5)71.5%	(5)71.5%	(5)71.5%
18 – Giving input on in-services	(4)50%	(4)50%	(4)50%	(4)50%	(4)50%	(4)50%

Chart 4 Classroom Procedures/Top questions of importance

Questions #	Gender	Race	Grades Taught	Years Experience	Type	Trained
20 – Appropriate classroom procedures	(8)100%	(8)100%	(8)100%	(8)100%	(8)100%	(8)100%
21 – Staff members to ask questions	(7)87.5%	(7)87.5%	(7)87.5%	(7)87.5%	(7)87.5%	(7)87.5%
22 – Office contact for emergencies	(7)87.5%	(7)87.5%	(7)87.5%	(7)87.5%	(7)87.5%	(7)87.5%
23 – Emergency drill procedures	(8)100%	(8)100%	(8)100%	(8)100%	(8)100%	(8)100%

CHAPTER FIVE

INTRODUCTION, SUMMARY OF THE STUDY, DISCUSSION OF

RESULTS AND CURRENT ISSUES, RECOMMENDATIONS, AND SUMMARY

Introduction

This study utilized a mixed method to gather data regarding the opinions and

thoughts of certified substitute teachers in a South Suburban school district of a Large

Metropolitan area and what they say is needed to be effective in the classroom. Training

programs for certified substitute teachers were researched and no information from the

perspective of the certified substitute teacher was found. The data collected from this

study is from the perspective of the certified substitute teacher. The certified substitute

teachers' perspective was investigated using a Likert scale questionnaire survey and an

open-ended question to fill a gap in the literature. Chapter 5 discusses the current

requirements for Substitute Teachers, implications of the study and recommendation for

further research.

Summary of the Study

This study was organized as an investigation of certified substitute teachers'

training programs and what the substitute teachers say is needed to be effective in the

classroom. The research design that was utilized for this study was a mixed methods

design that was developed by the researcher.

To construct a survey or questionnaire that would yield the information sought,

117

the developmental pattern of Koelling (1983) was followed to develop a survey suitable to gather the information needed for this study. Consultations with administrators were made to help generate a survey that would be relevant to the study that was conducted. Upon reviewing the survey instruments the questions were narrowed down to the general demographic questions in Part I and twenty-four (24) questions that made up Part II of the investigation part of the survey along with one open-ended question whereby certified substitutes could employ more insight.

Schools with training programs for certified substitute teachers were identified using data provided from the Illinois Board of Education Superintendent School Directory for the 2010-11 school year. The instrument created was later piloted in a South Suburban school district near a large metropolitan urban area. After receiving the results and percentages of what certified substitute teachers said they needed from training the instrument was considered suitable for information to be gathered from this study.

Out of sixteen school districts in the South Suburban area looked at only three school districts had a training program for certified substitute teachers. Some school districts looked at only had a 1-2-hour session while others had at least a half day of training. The school district chosen is study had a half a day substitute teacher orientation. Most school districts training focused on blood spills, cuts, airborne diseases, and other medical issues nothing really pertaining to a classroom and its function.

Certified substitute teachers were invited to come out and participate in this study. Not being allowed to communicate with the certified substitute teachers, by phone or via email, the school district was responsible for getting the word out. After working with the Human Resource Director, a flyer was generated that went out to all certified substitute teachers. The first two meeting dates set up after the Institutional Review Boards (IRB) approval were not until March, the Hunan Resource Director was out sick for several weeks. Despite setbacks the data collected was amazingly effective in answering the question "What do certify substitute teachers say is needed to be effective in the classroom?" This result was shared in Chapter 4.

The sample size turned out to be smaller than anticipated. There were to be approximately100 substitute teachers in the district substitute teacher pool. However, only seventy-five (75) notifications were sent out to certified substitute teachers to participate in the study. For population of 100 or less the entire population should be used in the sample. For a population of 500; 50% should be sampled. For 1,500 a sample of 20% should be used. For anything larger than 5,000 a percentage is irrelevant and about 400 for a sample should be sufficient (Leedy & Ormrod, 2005) The substitute teachers are the most likely candidates to supply this study with pertinent information as to what substitutes say is needed to be more effective in the classroom (McMillan, & Schumacher 2001).

Participation from all the substitute teachers was anticipated, unfortunately, only nine responded over a three-month period and eight completed the survey. Times were scheduled and meeting rooms were reserved one (1) day a week for three months. Participation was voluntary and there were no benefits for participating in the study.

The results in (Chapter 4) addressed what certified substitute teachers said is needed to be effective in the classroom. Upon analyzing the data, the twenty-four (24) questions were placed into four categories in which each question was coded to be place in one of the four categories. There are nine questions that were coded under the category of building procedures. Building procedures dealt with how certified substitute teachers felt about attending staff meetings, and district in-services where procedures are developed and disseminated to staff members. Having an administrator drop by throughout the day and giving feedback on performance were also listed as being of importance to certified substitute teachers. It was also said that understanding the bell schedule for individual grade levels or a master bell schedule for multiple grade level buildings is of great importance.

Feeling like a part of the staff and having an I.D. badge was also important to substitute teachers. These are simple things to fix. One can see how this would be important seeing in Chapter 2 (the Literature Review) there were complaints of substitutes not being treated fairly. It was also addressed in Chapter 4 with the open-ended question responses, where it was said, staff members and administrators were nasty and rude.

There were eight questions coded under the category of training. Even though the entire survey addressed what certified substitute teachers said was needed to be effective in the classroom these eight questions were specifically geared towards training to see what was lacking in the current training received by the certified substitute teachers. The top concerns of certified substitute teachers as it related to the questions on training are more training and how to deal with disruptive students. Most school districts including the one used in this study only had training for one day for the whole year.

Next, being trained on how to develop a classroom management plan ranked second in importance. These two could go hand in hand, if you have a classroom management plan more than likely there would be something on how to handle disruptive students. Training on how to develop a basic lesson and how to deliver instruction, also ranked in the top for certified substitute teachers. One should be able to understand why this would be of importance seeing that most certified substituted teachers have degrees in other areas than education and have not been properly trained to create or deliver lessons as comparable to that of a certified teacher that they are replacing for a day or longer.

121

The last two areas of training addressed are having more than one session of training per year and having the opportunity to give in-put in in-services. Even though this was last it was still of great importance to certified substitute teachers. This section alone validates the importance and need for the study based on what certified substitute teachers had to say about the training they would like to receive lets you know what is missing from what is already being done.

There were four questions coded under the category of classroom management. Again seeing that these are people who do not necessarily have the educational background to teach makes good sense for certified substitute teachers to need training on how to transition from one subject to another subject if they are replacing a teacher in a self-contained classroom where the teacher teaches all subjects not necessarily special education, but any regular class grades K-5. The same holds true for those transitioning from classroom to classroom certified substitute teachers need to know how to end a class to prepare for the next class without incident. The top issues in the classroom management section are how to keep students engaged in a lesson and when to make phone calls home. Making phone calls home can help or hurt a substitute teacher's credibility. You do not want to call immediately because the student will feel you do not have control of the classroom. However, by giving yourself time to handle a situation before calling home creates a rapport with the students and gives the substitute teacher credibility.

Finally, there were four questions that were coded under the category of classroom procedures. Classroom procedures are things that one should know to run the classroom in the absence of the regular classroom teacher. Knowing appropriate procedures to run the classroom and knowing a staff member to ask questions if needed. This information could be given by the substitute manager when the substitute arrives for an assignment, or it can be left in the plans left by the regular teacher. Knowing how to contact the office and knowing emergency drill procedures are classroom procedures that most people do not think are important, but it is important for the certified substitute teacher in the event of an emergency or a drill during a teacher absence. These are things one may not think of, but according to the survey certified substitute teachers say this is important and something they need to know to be more effective in the classroom.

Discussion

Cross tabulations of the demographics were done to see if there were any patterns in the way the different substitutes thought about training and what was needed to be effective in the classroom within the four categories that emerged from the questions on the survey.

In chart 1 you find gender, being male and female and the importance level for building procedures are extremely high. The majority believed attending building meetings and district in-services are incredibly important. This would make sense being that staff meetings and in-services are the venues used to train teachers, so why not utilize the same venue to train certified substitute teachers. Understanding the bell schedule feeling like a part of the staff and knowing appropriate building procedures are also incredibly important for both genders. Once again certified substitutes need to know when to release kids, so they do not play tricks on them. When you feel like a part of something you do a better job, you allow yourself to take ownership in what you are doing. Certified substitute teachers need to be able to take ownership of a classroom they are in otherwise they will never gain the respect needed to properly run a classroom.

Also, in chart 1 you will find race and for this study that constituted African Americans and White. The grade levels taught being K-8, their years of experience ranging from 1-10 or more years as a substitute teacher, the different types of substituting positions; day to day, floater, long term, short call, and permanent, and if they had gone through the district training program. All these variables produced the same level of importance for building procedures. There were slight variations, but not enough to change the overall importance for building procedures for certified substitute teachers.

Chart 2 deals with the training questions on the survey. Again, the same variables are used to generate percentages of importance. While seven questions stood out as having high importance three had the highest percentage for importance. How to handle disruptive behavior, how to plan a basic lesson and having more than one training session per year seemed to be most important when tabulated against all the variables.

Chart 3 addressed classroom management. Using the same variables making calls home, engaging students in the lesson and transitioning from subject to subject had the highest percentages for importance. Ironically, these three seem to go together, if you are busy making phone calls home you will lose the interest of students, whereby creating a setting in which students are not engaged and not allowing enough time to properly cover a subject. Classroom management is one of the key elements in being able to be effective in the classroom.

Chart 4 explains classroom procedures. It really did not surprise the researcher a whole lot when all four questions received high percentages from all six variables. Classroom procedures received the highest percentages out of all four categories, so the researcher believes the certified substitute teachers have spoken, what they need is more training in classroom procedures. To be effective anywhere you need to know what to do to do it.

125

Substitute teachers have been around for a long time. In most recent years substitute teachers have been needed more due to the increased number of out of district trainings for regular teachers. In Illinois for one to become a substitute teacher one just needed to have a bachelor's degree from an accredited four-year university in any field of study. According to the Will County Regional Office of Education (ROE), 2011 the requirements have changed slightly. To be a substitute teacher in the state of Illinois you must hold a valid teaching certificate or substitute certificate and you must have your certificate registered with the county in which you plan to teach. A substitute with a certificate may teach in place of a certified teacher for a maximum of 90 days in each district. A substitute certificate is only valid for four years, when a substitutes certificate expires, they must re-apply for a new one.

For someone to want to be a substitute teacher they must be dedicated and committed to go through the steps set aside for a substitute teacher in Illinois. Becoming a substitute teacher is not an easy process nor is it cheap. You must have the following:

- A degree from a four-year accredited university.
- Fill out an application complete with official transcripts to prove your degree.
- Pay $30.00 fee to state Superintendent of Education
- Pay $20.00 fee to register the certificate

New substitute teachers must go through a different process, as of January 1, 2011 seeking a substitute position in Illinois required the following:

- Register with the ROE and qualify for certification of Authorization in the county you wish to work.

- $49.00 initial fee for fingerprinting and criminal background check

- $20.00 to re-do fingerprints for State Level

- $25.00 to re-do fingerprints for Federal Level

- $49.00 to re-do fingerprints

- $10.00 document processing fee for out of county applicants for authorization registration

- $10.00 to re-print background check.

Before you can even get a certificate of Authorization you have to do the following:

- Submit Substitute Teacher Information form complete with physician statement and TB results

- Mandated Report Status

- Employment Eligibility Verification form 1-9 and two forms of I.D. in person

- Substitute Teacher Permission Form

- Physician Statement of good health and freedom from communicable disease signed by a physician no more than 90 days old

- $49.00 initial fee for criminal background check, as retrieved from

  http://www.willroe.org/SubstituteTeacher.html

Recommendations for Training Programs

To increase the effectiveness of substitute teachers in the classroom districts should consider the following to improve their training programs:

- Invite substitute teachers to attend staff meeting when they are substituting in the building on a building meeting day.

- Invest in your substitutes by allowing them to attend district in-services or have additional training for substitutes on those days that would help them be more effective in the classroom.

- Conduct more than one training session per year for substitute teachers.

- Trainings could be held at the beginning of the year, in the middle of the year, and at the end of the year to wrap thing up and generate topics for the coming year to train on.

- Allow substitutes to generate ideas for district in-services.

Recommendations for Future Research

Seeing that this topic has not been studied from the substitute teacher's perspective before gives researchers a window of opportunity to develop some even deeper thoughts into the topic. More studies are needed from the perspective of the substitute teacher and what is happening in the lines of training for substitute teachers. Some other topics to be researched are:

- An investigation of retention of substitute teachers. Currently with the stringent requirements. It would be good to know how many substitutes without a teacher's certificate go through the certification process over again after their four-year certificate expires.

- Conducting this study again with a larger sample of certified substitute teachers. To enhance the study some interviews may work better than the open-ended question.

- Conducting the same study using two or more school districts to compare if certified substitute teachers from different areas have the same thing to say about what is needed to be effective in the classroom.

- Conducting the study from the perspective of the students and what they say about their educational progress when a substitute is in the classroom.

- Conduct the study based on socioeconomic backgrounds of one or more

129

- schools to see if the results would be the same or not for certified substitutes teaching in different backgrounds
- Conduct a study based on race and certified substitute teachers and how views differ on what is thought to be important or needed in training for effectiveness in the classroom.

Summary

Having qualified teachers in the classroom has been a serious issue in this nation. Since the inception of The No Child Left Behind Act all teachers are required to be highly qualified (Wyld, 1995). What is highly qualified: a person well versed in the techniques that produce an effective classroom in which the educational process continues during the regular teacher's absence (Ballard, 2005). Honawar, 2007 stated less qualified substitute teachers were found in high poverty areas, which was interesting when looking at the different responses of African American and White substitute teachers in this study. There were several areas where White substitute teachers did not find them to be important when African American substitute teachers did. This could prove to be another problem in training substitute teachers.

Training practices for certified substitute teachers need to change. The same practices used for certified teachers need to be utilized in selecting substitute teachers. Another reason the research was done was to give certified substitute teachers a voice and to find out what they say is needed in training to be effective in the classroom instead of just putting a warm body in a classroom, a certified substitute teacher should be able to carry out the duties of the regular teacher. Being a certified teacher, this researcher tried to put all bias aside to focus on the greater good that would benefit the educational system.

131

APPENDIX A

Self-Administered Questionnaire Survey

An Investigation of Training Certified Substitute Teachers and what They Say I Needed

to Be Effective in The Classroom

APPENDIX A

SELF-ADMINISTERED QUESTIONNAIRE SURVEY

AN INVESTIGATION OF TRAINING CERTIFIED SUBSTITUTE TEACHERS AND WHAT THEY SAY IS NEEDED TO BE EFFECTIVE IN THE CLASSROOM

The purpose of this research is to investigate the training of certified substitute teachers from the perspective of what the certified substitute teachers' say is needed to be effective in the classroom. Your participation in this research study is strictly voluntary, and you may choose not to participate without fear of penalty or any negative consequences. Individual responses are anonymous; neither your name nor your district will be identified in the analysis. No individually identifiable information will be disclosed or published, and all results will be presented as aggregate, summary data. If you wish, you may request a summary of the results of this research by contacting the researcher through her email at ywalters@comcast.net. Please read all choices prior to marking your answers, some questions may require you to mark more than one answer.

PART I: GENERAL DEMOGRAPHICS

1. My gender is…

    ____Male   ____Female

2. My race is:

    ____ Black or African American ___White _____Asian ___American Indian or

    Alaskan Native ____Native Hawaiian or another Pacific Islander ____Other (Mixed

    Race)

3. Grades substituted for:

    _____ K-2 ____ 3-5 ____ 6-8 ___ All grades

4. Number of years substituting:

____ 1-3 years ____ 3-5 years ____ 5-7 years ____ 7-10 years ____10 or more years

5. Type of substituting done:

_____ Day to day ____ Floater (Substituting for more than one teacher in a day)

_____ Long term (21 Consecutive days) _____ Short Call (less than 14 days)

_____ All

6. Are you only a part of this districts substitute pool _____ Yes _____No, if no, how many other districts do you substitute for _____

7. Attendance of Substitute orientation in this district:

____ I have attended - **Please continue** with the Survey

____I have not attended – **Please STOP, DO NOT** continue with the survey

PART II: INVESTIGATION, SUBSTITUTE TEACHERS PERSPECTIVE

From your perspective as a substitute teacher, rate the importance level of each of the following statements relative to its impact on your effectiveness as a substitute. Choose the response number that best applies to each statement and record an X in the box to the right of the statement.

1=not important, 2=least important, 3= somewhat important, 4= important, 5= especially important

	1	2	3	4	5
1. Attending building meetings.					
2. Attending district in-services.					
3. Having administrative supervision throughout the day.					
4. Receiving written and/or verbal feedback on your performance.					
5. Having a written classroom management plan as part of the sub plan.					
6. Learning how to develop my own classroom management plan.					
7. Written strategies on how to handle disruptive students.					
8. Steps on how to determine the difference between minor/major infractions.					
9. Circumstances when it is appropriate to make phone calls home.					
10. How to plan a basic lesson.					
11. Guidelines on how to deliver instruction.					
12. Techniques to keep students attentive and engaged during a lesson.					
13. How to transition from classroom to classroom.					
14. How to transition from subject to subject.					
15. Knowing and understanding the bell schedule.					
16. Knowing and understanding the master building schedule.					
17. Attending more than one training session per year.					
18. Feeling like a part of the staff.					
19. Having an opportunity to give input on in-service needs.					
20. Knowing appropriate building procedures.					
21. Knowing appropriate classroom procedures.					
22. Knowing a staff member to ask questions if needed.					
23. Knowing how to contact the office in case of an emergency.					
24. Knowing the emergency drill procedures.					
25. Having an identification tag when substituting in the building.					

Please add any comments that you believe will clarify what substitute teachers need from training to be effective in the classroom.
Comments:

END OF QUESTIONNAIRE SURVEY You are now finished. Take some time to look over your responses to ensure you have answered every question. When you are done please return to the researcher. Thank you for your time and assistance.

APPENDIX B

Recruitment Script
An Investigation of Training Certified Substitute Teachers and what They Say Is Needed
to Be Effective
In the Classroom

137

APPENDIX B

RECRUITMENT SCRIPT

Hello, my name is Yvonne Henderson and I am a doctoral candidate at Argosy University Chicago campus. I am conducting a research study entitled: An Investigation of Training Certified Substitute Teachers and What They Say Is Needed to Be Effective in the Classroom. I have contacted your school district to obtain your assistance in helping with this research study. The following Informed Consent Form is written in first person to ensure the participants understand this information is geared to the participant and not the researcher. Any questions or concerns you may have the researcher is willing to address.

APPENDIX C

Informed Consent to Participate in Research

An Investigation of Training Certified Substitute Teachers and what They Say I Needed

to Be Effective in The Classroom

138

APPENDIX C

INFORMED CONSENT TO PARTICIPATE IN RESEARCH

AN INVESTIGATION OF TRAINING CERTIFIED SUBSTITUTE TEACHERS AND WHAT THEY SAY IS NEEDED TO BE EFFECTIVE IN THE CLASSROOM

Title of the Study
An Investigation of Training Certified Substitute Teachers and What They Say Is Needed to Be Effective in the Classroom

Introduction
Hello, my name is Yvonne Henderson and I am a doctoral candidate at Argosy University Chicago campus. I am conducting a research study entitled: An Investigation of Training Certified Substitute Teachers and What They Say Is Needed to Be Effective in the Classroom. I have contacted your school district to obtain your assistance in helping with this research study. The following Informed Consent Form is written in first person to ensure the participants understand this information is geared to the participant and not the researcher. Any questions or concerns you may have the researcher is willing to address.

Purpose of the Study
The purpose of this study is to investigate the training program of certified substitute teachers and to see what they say is needed to be effective in the classroom. There are approximately 100 substitute teachers from the district that will be asked to complete the self-administered questionnaire survey. The substitute teachers are the most likely candidates to supply this study with pertinent information as to what substitutes say is needed to be more effective in the classroom.

Statement of Consent

I understand participation in this study will require approximately twenty minutes of my time to complete the self-administered questionnaire survey. I understand this research will include approximately one-hundred substitute teachers from one school district. I understand if I agree to participate in this study, my signature on the Informed Consent Form confirms my willingness to participate in this study. I understand that I may obtain a copy of the signed Informed Consent Form from the principle investigator. I also understand that I will be asked to complete a self-administered survey because I have completed the district substitute training program. I understand that there will be no compensation of any kind for my participation in this study.

Initials _____   Date

_____

Risks and Benefits of Study

In this research, I understand there are no foreseeable or anticipated risks or benefits to me as a substitute teacher in this district or any other school district. The researcher realizes feelings may emerge from the survey questions and I do not have to respond to any questions which request information I am not comfortable revealing. There is no compensation offered for my participation. Upon requests from the district administrator an aggregate summary of data will be provided. Seeing that the researcher is not allowed to contact staff members due to the privacy act, the school district administrator will provide the participants with the research results if desired.

This research study will not have any participants that are minors, nor ask any questions that may require the reporting of child abuse or suicidal intent. In the event the principle investigator discovers any inappropriate behavior, criminal activity, or action that is required to be reported by law, the principle investigator will act according to the law and report the incident to the proper authority.

Your responses will provide a better understanding of how substitute training programs may be more effective for substitute teacher's effectiveness in the classroom.

Confidentially

I understand all information and data provided will be kept confidential and will be used for this research project only. The researcher's surveys will be highly guarded and privately maintained. All data will be stored in a locked file cabinet and data results will be confidentially maintained. Three years after the completion of the dissertation, the surveys and stored computerized data will be destroyed. The results of this research study may be published but my name and all individual responses will be confidential and neither my responses nor participation will be identified. All data from the surveys will be securely stored and accessible to the researcher only.

Participants Rights

I know that taking part in this study is completely voluntary. I may skip any questions that I do not want to answer. If I decide not to take part or to skip some of the questions, it will not affect my current or future relationship with the school district. If I decide to take part, I am free to withdraw at any time.

Initial _____   Date

_____

Questions or Problems

I understand and have read the above information, all questions have been answered satisfactorily and I voluntarily agree to participate in this research study. I understand the Institutional Review Board, Argosy University-Chicago has reviewed and certified this research study.

I further understand if I have any questions about this research study, I may contact the researcher and the researcher's faculty chairperson, whose contact information is provided below. I understand that if I have research questions or related problems concerning participant's

rights, I may contact the Institutional Review Board through the IRB Chair, David Van Dyke, Dyke@argosy.edu 312-777-7600.

Researcher

Yvonne Henderson   Email Address: drhenderson77@gmail.com

708-724-6426

Faculty Chairperson

Dr. Deborah Hammond-Watts   Email Address: <u>dhammond-</u>
<u>watts@edmc.edu</u>

(Office) 225 N. Michigan Avenue, 13th Floor

 Chicago, IL 60601

Participant Signature

Participant's Name (Printed) _____

Signature: _____ Date_____

Signature Researcher: _____Date_____

APPENDIX D

Permission Letter, Harvey School District 152

An Investigation of Training Certified Substitute Teachers and what They Say Is Needed
to Be Effective
In the Classroom

HARVEY PUBLIC SCHOOLS
DISTRICT NUMBER 152

DISTRICT ADMINISTRATION
Eric J. Kellogg
Superintendent of Schools
Thorne W. Humphrey
Director of Business
Operations

Ankhe Bradley
Director of Human Resources
Personnel
Denise Braggs Brown
Director of Special Services
Lisa Scolaro
Director of Curriculum and
Technology

BOARD OF EDUCATION
Tyrone Rogers
President
Gloria Johnson
Vice President
Linda Hawkins
Secretary
Keith Price
Member
George Robinson
Member
Joyce Kellogg-Weaver
Member
Betty Johnson
Member

July 28, 2010

Argosy University Institutional Review Board
Chicago, Campus
225 North Michigan Avenue
Suite 1300
Chicago, Illinois 60601

TO WHOM IT MAY CONCERN:

Ms. Yvonne Henderson, Argosy University doctoral candidate, has requested the participation of our Certified Substitute Teachers Program. Ms. Henderson will be permitted to survey the Certified Substitute Teachers for this research at our facility or at a mutually agreed upon site.

Ms. Henderson will contact the Superintendent or Lisa Sharpe according to the date and time of availability. We are requesting Yvonne Henderson to provide a copy of the Argosy University IRB-approved, stamped consent document before any surveys are distributed.

I look forward to helping Ms. Yvonne Henderson successfully complete her research requirement.

If there is any information required please contact me at: 708-333-0300 X14

Sincerely,

Eric J. Kellogg
Superintendent

cc. Yvonne Henderson

APPENDIX E

CITI Collaborative Institutional Completion Report

An Investigation of Training Certified Substitute Teachers and what They Say Is Needed
to Be Effective
In the Classroom

CITI Collaborative Institutional Training Initiative

AU Students Curriculum Completion Report
Printed on 8/7/2010

Learner: Yvonne Henderson (username: yhenderson)
Institution: Argosy University
Contact
Information
332 Mohawk, St.
Park Forest, Illinois 60466 USA
Phone: 708-724-6426
Email: ywalters@comcast.net

AU Students:

Stage 1. Basic Course Passed on 08/07/10 (Ref # 4739094)

Required Modules	Date Completed	Score
History and Ethical Principles - SBR	08/07/10	4/4 (100%)
Assessing Risk in Social and Behavioral Sciences - SBR	08/07/10	5/5 (100%)
Informed Consent - SBR	08/07/10	5/5 (100%)
Argosy University	08/07/10	no quiz

For this Completion Report to be valid, the learner listed above must be affiliated with a CITI participating institution. Falsified information and unauthorized use of the CITI course site is unethical, and may be considered scientific misconduct by your institution.

Paul Braunschweiger Ph.D.
Professor, University of Miami
Director Office of Research Education
CITI Course Coordinator

Return

APPENDIX F

Institutional Review Board Approval

An Investigation of Training Certified Substitute Teachers and what They Say Is Needed
to Be Effective
In the Classroom

147

ARGOSY
UNIVERSITY.

IRB CERTIFICATION LETTER

Yvonne Henderson

Re: IRB Protocol #: 756

Your study entitled **"An Investigation of Training Certified Substitute Teachers and What They Say is Needed to be Effective in the Classroom"** has been *certified* on **1/4/11** by the Institutional Review Board, Argosy University, **Chicago Campus**. You may now proceed with your research project, following the protocol that was certified by the IRB.

Your certification is valid through **1/3/12**. If you wish to continue with your study beyond that date, a Continuing Certification of Compliance Form (Appendix P of the IRB Handbook) must be submitted to and certified by the IRB.

Your research must be conducted according to the protocol that was certified by the IRB, and any changes to the protocol must be reported to and Certified by the IRB before the changes may be implemented. You must report any adverse events or reactions to the IRB.

All participants should be provided with a copy of the informed consent document Certified by the IRB for use in this study.

Please contact our office with any questions. All future correspondence must include the IRB protocol number and the title of the study.

Sincerely,

The Institutional Review Board
Argosy, Chicago

CC: Dr. Deborah Hammond-Watts, Dissertation Chair

Reference

Ballard, M. (2005). One district's experience in creating an effective substitute training program.

    SubJournal, 6(1), 40-47. Retrieved from http://web.ebsohost.com/ehost/delivery

Dyri, O.E. (2004). Sub-Ways. Retrieved from www.DistrictAdministration.com

Ezarik, M. (2004). The substitute game. *District Administrator, 40*(7), 30-35. Retrieved

    from EBSCO database.

Fink, A. (1995). How to ask survey questions. Thousand Oaks, CA: SAGE Publications.

Fielder, D. (1991). An examination of substitute teacher effectiveness. *Clearing House, 64*(6),

    375. Retrieved from http://web.ebscohost.com/ehost/delivery

Gentry, K. M. (2005). The journey of an education service center into the

    development of an effective substitute teachers training program. *SubJournal,*

    6(1), 28-34. Retrieved from http://web.ebscohost.com/ehost/delivery

Guskey, T., & Sparks, D. (1991). What to consider when evaluating staff development.

    Educational Leadership, 49(3), 73-76.

Haines, B. (2005). A quick check on the pulse of substitute teacher management. *SubJournal,* 6

    (1), 35-39. Retrieved from http://web.ebscohost.com/ehost/delivery

Henderson, Y. (2010). Self-Administered survey: An investigation of training certified substitute teachers and what they say is needed to be effective in the classroom.

Honawar, V. (2007). Policies allow districts to cut corners with substitutes. Retrieved

   from http://web.ebscohost.com/ehost/delivery

Illinois Board of Education. (2010). Illinois Board of Education Superintendent School
Directory

   for the 2010-11 school year.

Jehlen, A. (2004). Super-subs. *NEA Today, 22*(8), 1-3. Retrieved from

   http://web.ebscohost.com/ehost/delivery

Javernick, E. (2005). A hand to substitutes. *Teaching PreK-8, 36*(2), 47. Retrieved from

   http://web.ebscohost.come/ehost/delivery

Jones, K. R. (1999). Managing substitute teachers. *Here's How, 18*(2) 1-5. Retrieved

   from http://web.ebscohost.com/ehost/delivery

Keller, B. (2004). Denver substitute teachers slam proposal to cut pay by two-thirds.
Education

   Week, 24(2), 4. Retrieved from http://web.ebscohost.com/ehost/delivery

Koelling, C. H. (1983). Substitute teachers – School policies and procedures in the north
central

   region. *Education, 104*(2), 155-171.

King James Version. 2011. The Holy Bible. Iowa Falls, IA. World Bible Publishers, Inc.

Lamarque, E. (2005). St. Tammy parish on the move from good to great. *SubJournal*,

6(1), 9-16.

Retrieved from http://web.ebscohost.com/ehost/delivery

Lassmann, M. E. (2001). Defining the role of the substitute teacher. *Education, 121*(3), 625-628.

 Retrieved from Academic Search Complete database.

Leedy, P. D. & Ormrod, J. E. (2005). Practical research: Planning and design. (8th Ed.). Upper Saddle River, New Jersey: Pearson Education, Inc.

McMillian, J., & Schumacher, S. (2001). *Research in education.* New York: Addison Wesley Lognman.

NEA. (2010). National Education Association.com

Nidds, J., & McGerald, J. (1994). Substitute teachers: Seeking meaningful instruction in the teacher's absence. *Clearing House, 68*(1), 25. Retrieved from Academic Search Complete Database.

Patton, M. Q. (2002). Qualitative research & evaluation methods. (3rd Ed.). Thousand Oaks, California: Sage Publication, Inc.

Purvis, J. & Garvey, R. (1993). Components of an effective substitute teacher program. *Clearing House, 66* (6), 370. Retrieved from Academic Search Complete Database.

Shaw, J. B. (1998). How to create a "gruntled" substitute. Retrieved from www.TeachingK-12.com

Shepherd, R. (1997). Formative assessment for substitute teacher *Clearing House, 71*(2),

117. Retrieved from Academic Search Complete database.

Substitute Teaching Institution at Utah State University. (2010). Retrieved from
www.stiusu.com

Tannebaum, M. D. (2000). No substitute for quality. *Educational Leadership*, *57*(8), 70-

72. Retrieved from http://ebscohost.com/ehost/delivery

University of Wisconsin EAU CLAIRE. (2009). *Data collection methods.* Retrieved from

http://people.uwec.edu/piercech/ResearchMethods/Data%20collection%20method

s/DATA%20COLLECTION%20METHODS.htm

Warner, B. (2003). Lessons for a substitute teacher: Recalling the line plot amid paper

waddings.

Concept. Retrieved from EBSCO database.

Webster. 2010. Webster's new world college dictionary. Cleveland, Ohio. Wiley

Publishing, Inc.

Will County Regional Board of Education. Retrieved from

http://www.willroe.org/SubstituteTeacher.html

Wyld, D. C. (1995). The FMLA and the changing demand for substitute teachers.

Clearing House, *68*(5) 301-306. Retrieved from

http://ebscohost.com/ehost/delivery

www.ingramcontent.com/pod-product-compliance
Lightning Source LLC
Chambersburg PA
CBHW080623030426
42336CB00018B/3060